'Lea Getu's work offers powerful insights into the taboo of female sexual abuse and clearly outlines the impact on therapists who encounter survivors and perpetrators. Based on her meticulous research, this beautifully written and highly original book should be essential reading for clinicians.'

Dr Anna Motz, *Consultant Clinical and Forensic Psychologist, working for CNWL Health and Justice Services, Author and Psychoanalytic Psychotherapist*

'This is a groundbreaking and urgently needed book. I was struck by how clearly and compassionately it tackles a subject so often left in the shadows. The author brings in-depth clinical insights to the complex dynamics of female-to-female child sexual abuse, offering guidance that is illuminating, practical, and thought-provoking. It challenges how we think about survivors and perpetrators alike. A very important read for anyone working in this field.'

Richard Curen, *Forensic Psychotherapist and Chair of the Forensic Psychotherapy Society*

'Getu's compelling work shines a light on what many may view as a taboo subject. Her sensitive and courageous exploration of female-to-female child sexual abuse, interweaving the professional and the personal, and formulating the concept of bold empathy as central to the therapeutic work, makes a significant and original contribution to a little researched area.'

Dr Jessica Yakeley, *Director, Portman Clinic, Tavistock and Portman NHS Foundation Trust*

'This is a powerful and bold work in which Dr. Getu courageously explores a domain of therapy that is not often discussed; namely psychodynamic psychotherapy with female perpetrators of sexual abuse of children. The book is unique in that it offers accounts of what makes women abuse children this way and also offers accounts of what it feels like to be a therapist doing such work. Getu rightly emphasises the importance of boundaries in the work and the value of supervision and working in teams. This work will be essential reading for any therapist thinking of working with female perpetrators of sexual violence.'

Dr Gwen Adshead, *Forensic Psychiatrist and Psychotherapist*

'This powerful and courageous book offers a rare blend of emotional depth and theoretical clarity. A must-read for clinicians and students alike, it introduces "bold empathy" – a vital, fresh lens for working with complex clients.'

Heidi Ahonen, PhD, RP, *Trauma Psychotherapist, Professor, Coordinator of PhD Programme, Wilfrid Laurier University, Canada*

Therapeutic Work with Perpetrators and Survivors of Female-to-Female Child Sexual Abuse

This book provides a guide to working with survivors and perpetrators of female-to-female child sexual abuse (F-FCSA), examining the clinical challenges of treating perpetrators and survivors of F-FCSA and how to overcome them.

Divided into two parts, the first part of this book sets F-FCSA in its historical, societal, and intra-psychic context, reviewing why some women abuse children, the barriers to recognising this, and the prevalence of F-FCSA. The second part sets out ways to work more effectively with survivors and perpetrators by drawing from in-depth interviews with prominent therapists working in the field. Topics addressed include working with extreme splitting, enmeshment, and integration; complex countertransference and transference; recognising embodied feelings; and processing the extreme impacts of the work on the therapist and the therapeutic relationship. Through the heartfelt voices of the therapists and clinical case studies, this book teaches clinicians how to manage the extreme emotions evoked by difficult narratives and behaviours of the clients and how to have a new and deeper understanding of empathy as the key within this difficult work.

This is an important read for clinical psychologists, psychotherapists, forensic psychotherapists, counsellors, social workers, and other professionals working with this client group.

Lea Getu, PhD, is an integrative psychotherapist and a registered member of UKCP who has worked within primary care, colleges, and in private practice for over 20 years. She is also an Assistant Professor and the foundation course leader of the Psychotherapy and Counselling Foundation Certificate at Regent's University, London.

The Forensic Psychotherapy Monograph Series

The Official Publication Series of the International Association for Forensic Psychotherapy

Series Editor: Professor Brett Kahr

For further information about this series please visit https://www.routledge.com/The-Forensic-Psychotherapy-Monograph-Series/book-series/KARNFPM

Therapeutic Work with Perpetrators and Survivors of Female-to-Female Child Sexual Abuse

A Clinician's Guide

Lea Getu

Routledge
Taylor & Francis Group

LONDON AND NEW YORK

Designed cover image: Getty images

First published 2026
by Routledge
4 Park Square, Milton Park, Abingdon, Oxon OX14 4RN

and by Routledge
605 Third Avenue, New York, NY 10158

Routledge is an imprint of the Taylor & Francis Group, an informa business

For Product Safety Concerns and Information please contact our
EU representative GPSR@taylorandfrancis.com. Taylor & Francis
Verlag GmbH, Kaufingerstraße 24, 80331 München, Germany.

British Library Cataloguing-in-Publication Data
A catalogue record for this book is available from the British Library

ISBN: 978-1-032-99980-7 (hbk)
ISBN: 978-1-032-99978-4 (pbk)
ISBN: 978-1-003-60700-7 (ebk)

DOI: 10.4324/9781003607007

Typeset in Times New Roman
by codeMantra

To my husband Makonen, and my children Judit, Hiwot, and Yoshu

Contents

Acknowledgements

I would like to thank from the bottom of my heart all the courageous clinicians I interviewed for my PhD and who gave their permission to use the material gained from it for any further publications, including a book. Without them, this book, specifically the second section, would not exist. Their intimate experiences and insights are invaluable, and I believe will help many other clinicians to manage their work more effectively when working with female-to-female child sexual abuse (F-to-FCSA).

I owe thanks to numerous clinicians and authors who have written about FCSA, whose work has helped me to understand the complexities of F-to-FCSA, and whose significant knowledge I have drawn from in various parts of this book. I especially want to thank Dr. Estela Welldon for her groundbreaking work within the area of FCSA, which changed my life in so many ways.

I want to thank Professor Brett Kahr, the editor of the Karnack Forensic Series. He saw the potential in this book and enabled it to happen. I thank him for his kindness and encouragement all the way through this book project.

I want to thank the editorial team at Routledge for being extremely supportive and helpful.

I remain indebted to Dr. Anna Motz for her enduring support and for guiding me through the analysis of the interviewed therapists with such sensitivity and wisdom. I cannot thank her enough.

I also thank my friends Dr. Ravi and Elizabeth Knight, Amelia Jeans, Dr. Silvia Elsner, Harriet and Frank Matsaert (MBE), Leif Danielsson, Shitaye Haile Lemma, and Dr. Lemma Degefa for encouraging me to write this book.

I thank my sisters, Tuula Miettunen and Seija Korkeamaki, who have given me warmth and sisterly love throughout my journey. I also thank my brother-in-law, Kari Miettunen, for his kindness and support.

With great love, I want to thank my loving husband, Makonen, for always believing in me. His comments and sharp scholarship skills have been a great sounding board throughout this project.

And with heartfelt love, I thank my daughter, Judit Getu, for editing this book and offering me her brilliant language skills. Working with my daughter has been a wonderful experience as she has understood my cognitive and emotional language through and through.

I will always thank my late parents: my mother Terttu, for her love for the eight years she was with me and for giving me a singing voice to express all the colours imaginable, and my father Pentti, for showing me how to enter a painting and fly beyond.

And my grandchildren – you give me life and love!

Series editor's foreword

In 1801, the English judiciary condemned a 13-year-old boy to death and then hanged him on the gallows at Tyburn, in the heart of London. But what crime had he committed? Apparently, this young lad had stolen merely a spoon (Westwick, 1940). Tragically, during the early nineteenth century, such an infraction could actually result in capital punishment.

Throughout much of human history, our ancestors have performed rather poorly when responding to acts of violence. In most cases, our predecessors will either have *ignored* murderousness, as in the case of Graeco-Roman infanticide, which occurred so regularly in the ancient world that it acquired an almost normative status (deMause, 1974; Kahr, 1994); or they will have *punished* destructible behaviours with retaliatory sadism – a form of unconscious identification with the aggressor. Any history of criminology will readily reveal the cruel punishments inflicted upon prisoners throughout the ages, ranging from beatings and stockades to more severe forms of torture, culminating in eviscerations, lynchings, beheadings, and electrocutions (e.g., Kahr, 2020, 2022, 2025).

Only during the last 100 years have we begun to develop the capacity to respond more intelligently and more humanely to dangerousness and destruction. Since the advent of psychoanalysis, we now have access to a much deeper understanding of both the aetiology of aggressive acts and their treatment; and, fortunately, we need no longer ignore criminals or abuse them – instead, we can offer forensic psycho-therapeutic interventions with compassion and containment, as well as conduct research which can help to prevent future acts of violence. By *treating* sadistic patients, rather than by *punishing* them, forward-thinking mental health practition-ers now possess the ability to draw upon the new discipline of forensic psycho-therapy, designed to understand the causes of violence, in order to help rehumanise the dehumanised.

The discipline of forensic psychotherapy can trace its origins to the very early days of psychoanalysis. On 6 February 1907, at a meeting of the Wiener Psycho-analytische Vereinigung [Vienna Psycho-Analytical Society], Professor Sigmund Freud bemoaned the often horrible treatment of mentally ill offenders. Accord-ing to Herr Otto Rank, Freud's secretary at the time, the founder of psychoanaly-sis, expressed his sorrow at the 'unsinnige Behandlung dieser Leute' (quoted in

Rank, 1907a: 101), which translates as the 'nonsensical treatment of these people' (quoted in Rank, 1907b: 108).

Subsequently, many of the early psychoanalytical practitioners preoccupied themselves with forensic topics. Dr. Hanns Sachs, himself a trained lawyer, and the Princesse Marie Bonaparte, a noted French aristocrat, spoke fiercely against capital punishment. Sachs, one of the first members of Freud's inner circle, regarded the death penalty for offenders as an example of group sadism (Moellenhoff, 1966), while Bonaparte (1927), who had studied various murderers throughout her career, actually campaigned to free the convicted killer Caryl Chessman during his sentence on Death Row at the California State Prison in San Quentin (Bertin, 1982).

Some years later, Mrs. Melanie Klein (1932a), the Austrian-born, British-based clinician, concluded her first book, the landmark text *Die Psychoanalyse des Kindes* – known in English as *The Psycho-Analysis of Children* (Klein, 1932b) – with a truly memorable clarion call. Mrs. Klein noted that acts of criminality stem invariably from disturbances in childhood and that if young people could receive psychoanalytical treatment at an early age, then much cruelty would be prevented in later years. As she argued, 'If every child who shows disturbances that are at all severe were to be analysed in good time, a great number of these people who later end up in prisons or lunatic asylums, or who go completely to pieces, would be saved from such a fate and be able to develop a normal life'[1] (Klein, 1932b: 374).

Shortly after the publication of Klein's transformative book, Atwell Westwick, a judge of the Superior Court of Santa Barbara, California, published a little-known, though highly inspiring, article on 'Criminology and Psychoanalysis' in *The Psychoanalytic Quarterly*. Westwick may well be the first judge to have committed himself in print to the value of psychoanalysis in the study of criminality, arguing that punishment of the forensic patient remains, in fact, a sheer waste of time. With passion, Judge Westwick (1940: 281) queried, 'Can we not, in our well nigh hopeless and overwhelming struggle with the problems of delinquency and crime, profit by medical experience with the problems of health and disease? Will we not, eventually, terminate the senseless policy of sitting idly by until misbehavior occurs, often with irreparable damage, then dumping the delinquent into the juvenile court or reformatory and dumping the criminal into prison?' Westwick noted that we should, instead, train judges, probation officers, social workers, as well as teachers and parents, in the precepts of psychoanalysis, in order to arrive at a more sensitive, non-punitive understanding of the nature of criminality. As Westwick (1940: 281) opined, 'When we shall have succeeded in committing society to such a program, when we see it launched definitely upon the venture, as in time it surely will be – then shall we have erected an appropriate memorial to Sigmund Freud'.

Although the roots of forensic psychotherapy stem back to the early years of the twentieth century (e.g., Kahr, 2018, 2022, 2025), the discipline did not become constellated more formally until the 1980s and 1990s, due, in large measure, to the pioneering work of the esteemed forensic psychiatrist and forensic psychotherapist, Dr. Estela Valentina Welldon (1988, 1996, 2002, 2011, 2015), and many of her colleagues; and, thankfully, the profession now boasts a much more robust foundation, with training courses available for young mental health workers in the United Kingdom and beyond. Since the inauguration of the Diploma in Forensic Psychotherapy, created by Dr. Welldon, hosted by the Portman Clinic in London, and sponsored by the British Postgraduate Medical Federation of the University of London, with the support and encouragement of its leader, Professor Sir Michael Peckham (Kahr, 2021), students can now seek further instruction in the psychodynamic treatment of patients who act out in a dangerous and illegal manner. Dr. Welldon – subsequently Profesora Welldon – created not only the world's first training programme in forensic psychotherapy, but she also launched the International Association for Forensic Psychotherapy in 1991 and hosted its inaugural conference in 1992 at St. Bartholomew's Hospital in London. This passionate and devoted organisation has certainly helped to develop the field globally.

Back in 1997, at the kind invitation of Mr. Cesare Sacerdoti, the owner of H. Karnac (Books) at that time, I had the privilege of commissioning a host of titles for a new book series designed to promote this growing branch of forensic psychological assessment, treatment, and prevention; and the very first titles appeared several years later (Bloom, 2001; Kahr, 2001; Saunders, 2001). Over time, this 'Forensic Psychotherapy Monograph Series', now published by Routledge, part of the Taylor and Francis Group, has endeavoured to produce a regular stream of high-quality titles, written by leading members of the profession, who share their expertise in a concise and practice-orientated fashion. We trust that this collection of books, which, in 2022, became the official monograph series of the International Association for Forensic Psychotherapy, will help to consolidate and to disseminate the knowledge and experience that we have already acquired and will also provide more creative pathways in the decades to come.

Happily, our growing field of forensic psychotherapy boasts many creative and productive colleagues, not least Dr. Lea Getu, a very experienced psychotherapist and academic who has taught for many years at Regent's University London and who holds the post of Assistant Professor and also that of the university's popular Foundation Course Leader of the Psychotherapy and Counselling Foundation Certificate. Based upon her extensive research, Getu has strongly expanded the pioneering achievements of the aforementioned Profesora Estela Valentina Welldon, one of the very first mental health professionals who had dared to highlight the horrors of sexual abuse perpetrated by *women*, as well as by men. Thankfully, in this new book, *Therapeutic Work with Perpetrators and Survivors of Female-to-Female Child Sexual Abuse: A Clinician's Guide*, Lea Getu has generously shared her many interviews with fellow practitioners who have studied female-to-female child sexual abuse – rendered acronymically as 'F-FCSA' – with great care and great professionalism.

Back in the 1980s, I enjoyed the great privilege of having trained with Estela Welldon at the Portman Clinic in London, and I shall never forget how her inaugural book, *Mother, Madonna, Whore: The Idealization and Denigration of Motherhood*, released in 1988, shocked so many colleagues, most of whom believed that only *men* would dare to assault children. Fortunately, Lea Getu has enhanced

Welldon's brave insights, and she has now provided us with innumerable new theories about how and why and when the mothers of children would dare to attack their own offspring in such a sadistic manner.

I deeply admire Lea Getu's tremendous bravery in confronting this terrifying material in such a blunt, honest, and well-processed manner. Indeed, we should consider ourselves very honoured to include this important text by Dr. Getu in our 'Forensic Psychotherapy Monograph Series'. And we must all come to appreciate that, by speaking honestly about the commonality of violence not only in men but also in women, we might therefore become better able to identify people at risk of sexual assault sooner rather than later and thus help to reduce the prospect of assaults through early psychotherapeutic interventions.

As the new millennium begins to unfold, we now have an opportunity for psychotherapeutically inclined forensic mental health professionals to work in close conjunction with child psychologists and with infant mental health specialists so that the problems of violence can be tackled not only retrospectively but also preventatively. With the growth of the field of forensic psychotherapy, we at last have reason to be hopeful that serious criminality can be forestalled and, perhaps, one day, even eradicated.

Professor Brett Kahr.
Series Editor, 'Forensic Psychotherapy Monograph Series', International Association for Forensic Psychotherapy.
Adviser-in-Chief, Forensic Psychotherapy Society.
Member, Board of Trustees, International Association for Forensic Psychotherapy.

Note

1 The original German phrase reads: 'Würde jedes Kind, das ernstere Störungen zeigt, rechtzeitig der Analyse unterzogen, dann könnte wohl ein großer Teil jener Menschen, die andernfalls in Gefängnissen und Irrenhäusern landen oder sonst völlig scheitern, vor diesem Schicksal bewahrt bleiben und sich zu normalen Menschen entwickeln' (Klein, 1932a: 293).

Bibliography

Bertin, C. (1982) *La Dernière Bonaparte*. Paris: Librairie Académique Perrin.

Bloom, S.L. (ed.) (2001) *Violence: A Public Health Menace and a Public Health Approach*. London: H. Karnac (Books).

Bonaparte, M. (1927) Le Cas de Madame Lefebvre. *Revue Française de Psychanalyse*, 1, pp. 149–198.

deMause, L. (1974) 'The evolution of childhood', in deMause, L. (ed.) *The History of Childhood*. New York: Psychohistory Press, pp. 1–73.

Kahr, B. (1994) 'The historical foundations of ritual abuse: An excavation of ancient infanticide', in Sinason, V. (ed.) *Treating Survivors of Satanist Abuse*. London: Routledge, pp. 45–56.

Kahr, B. (ed.) (2001) *Forensic Psychotherapy and Psychopathology: Winnicottian Perspectives*. London: H. Karnac (Books).

Kahr, B. (2018) '"No intolerable persons" or "lewd pregnant women": Towards a history of forensic psychoanalysis', in Kahr, B. (Ed.) *New Horizons in Forensic Psychotherapy: Exploring the Work of Estela V. Welldon*. London: Karnac Books, pp. 17–87.

Kahr, B. (2020) *Dangerous Lunatics: Trauma, Criminality, and Forensic Psychotherapy*. London: Confer / Confer Books.

Kahr, B. (2021) Professor Sir Michael Peckham: A memorial tribute. *International Journal of Forensic Psychotherapy*, 3, pp. 163–165.

Kahr, B. (2022) "Let the great axe fall": From ancient Babylonian torture to modern forensic psychotherapy. Freud, Welldon, and the humanisation of criminality. *International Journal of Forensic Psychotherapy*, 4, pp. 89–118.

Kahr, B. (2025) *Forensic Psychoanalysis: From Sub-Clinical Psychopaths to Serial Killers*. London: Routledge / Taylor and Francis Group, and Abingdon: Routledge / Taylor and Francis Group.

Klein, M. (1932a) *Die Psychoanalyse des Kindes*. Vienna: Internationaler Psychoanalytischer Verlag.

Klein, M. (1932b) *The Psycho-Analysis of Children*. Trans. Strachey, A. London: Hogarth Press and the Institute of Psycho-Analysis.

Moellenhoff, F. (1966) 'Hanns Sachs. 1881–1947: The creative unconscious', in Alexander, F., Eisenstein, S. and Grotjahn, M. (eds.) *Psychoanalytic Pioneers*. New York: Basic Books, pp. 180–199.

Rank, O. (ed.) (1907a) 'Vortragsabend: Am 6. Februar 1907', in Nunberg, H. and Federn, E. (eds.) *Protokolle der Wiener Psychoanalytischen Vereinigung: Band I. 1906–1908*. Frankfurt am Main: S. Fischer / S. Fischer Verlag, pp. 97–104.

Rank, O. (ed.) (1907b) 'Scientific meeting on February 6, 1907', in Nunberg, H. and Federn, E. (eds.) *Minutes of the Vienna Psychoanalytic Society: Volume I: 1906–1908*. Trans. Nunberg, M. New York: International Universities Press, pp. 103–110.

Saunders, J.W. (ed.) (2001) *Life within Hidden Walls: Psychotherapy in Prisons*. London: H. Karnac (Books).

Welldon, E.V. (1988) *Mother, Madonna, Whore: The Idealization and Denigration of Motherhood*. London: Free Association Books.

Welldon, E.V. (1996) 'Contrasts in male and female sexual perversions', in Cordess, C. and Cox, M. (eds.) *Forensic Psychotherapy: Crime, Psychodynamics and the Offender Patient. Volume II. Mainly Practice*. London: Jessica Kingsley Publishers, pp. 273–289.

Welldon, E.V. (2002) *Sadomasochism*. Cambridge: Icon Books.

Welldon, E.V. (2011) *Playing with Dynamite: A Personal Approach to the Psychoanalytic Understanding of Perversions, Violence, and Criminality*. London: Karnac Books.

Welldon, E. (2015) Forensic psychotherapy. *Psychoanalytic Psychotherapy*, 29, pp. 211–227.

Westwick, A. (1940) Criminology and psychoanalysis. *Psychoanalytic Quarterly*, 9, pp. 269–282.

Introduction

In the beginning

Untitled poem (Lea Getu, 1976)

Inside me
Lives an aggressive loneliness

Loneliness
Like
Dismantled arms
Like
Head separated from its mother-body
Like
Feet so paralysed and still

Yet running

Wrapping my arms around
My soaring being
Squeezing
Crushingly embracing

To feel
The split body
The body

I wrote the above poem as a teenager. My young adulthood was marked by an incessant weight of feeling greatly isolated, lonely, and confused. I had no access route available to me through which I could understand the sexual abuse, nor its context, and the ensuing trail of trauma that had been inflicted on me as an eight-year-old child by my mother-figure. While this poem describes my aching sense of being cut-off from my emotions, body, and environment, it also depicts a picture of splits occupying larger bodies within our world. This cut-offness is present on a societal level as well as being present among clinicians when faced with the phenomena

DOI: 10.4324/9781003607007-1

of female-to-female child sexual abuse (F-to-FCSA). The divisions caused by F-to-FCSA, within and between victims, perpetrators, society, and professionals, are indisputably tangible and are explored in numerous ways and levels in this book.

As a child and a teenager, I would seek solace and refuge in Finnish nature, God, and my poems. They became my companions and my comforters, providing me with strength. I spoke only to and through them about my sense of lostness. The poems I wrote kept me alive.

The aim of this book

When I finally realised what had happened to me, I started searching for answers to the questions I had been carrying: Why do some females end up abusing children? How are daughters/girls impacted by being sexually abused by a mother or a female figure? And later, when I became a psychotherapy student, I started asking – what do we know about the history of female child sexual abuse (FCSA) and the theories related to it? As part of my MA thesis (2003) titled 'An Exploration of Female-to-Female Child Sexual Abuse', I interviewed survivors of F-to-FCSA. The research findings of that enquiry were solely predicated on the lived experiences of the survivors, and some of these findings have been incorporated into this book. It was during my MA research that I began to realise that there was a clear gap within the existing research on F-to-FCSA.

I found myself traversing a limiting landscape where I struggled to find any substantive research around the clinical experiences of therapists working in the field of F-to-FCSA. This realisation cultivated a yearning within me to do my part in narrowing the gap, and it was through embarking on my PhD research that I was able to bring this mission to life.

My PhD research (2019) titled 'An Exploration of Complexities of Therapeutic Work with Female-to-Female Child Sexual Abuse' became a solidifying pathway in the sense that it began to answer the many unresolved questions that I had related to F-to-FCSA. While these questions were originally investigated and answered in an academic context, this book is intended to provide a more reader-friendly version with an additional case study (Chapter 3).

This book is largely based on the findings of my PhD research and, specifically, the enriching discoveries from the examined interviews of the six therapists I conducted. The methodology I applied for the analysis of the interviews was interpretative phenomenological analysis (IPA) as described by Smith et al. (2009). Although it does not elaborate on how IPA was used to reach the results of the analyses, the analyses in this book do form the main bulk of Part II – 'Clinical Implications'. The research question that guided the field study was: What is the participant's (therapist's) experience of working with F-to-FCSA, and what are the issues related to it? To get an answer to that inquiry, the six therapists that I interviewed were asked the following questions:

1   Could you tell me about your experience working with female-to-female child sexual abuse?

2 How has working with female-to-female child sexual abuse impacted your personal life?
3 What is your framework for understanding female child sexual abuse?
4 What motivates you to go on working in this area?
5 Anything else you want to add?

Before introducing the chapters, it is important to clarify what this book is not about. It is not: (i) a clinical research dealing with the question of whether female sexual offenders are mentally ill and/or addicted to substances, (ii) a research into the prevalence of female sexual offending, (iii) an in-depth exploration of the categorisation of female sex offenders, (iv) exploring how to assess the perpetrators or the survivors of the F-to-FCSA, (v) investigating how to stop recidivism, (vi) exploring possible data of F-to-FCSA in various cultural contexts, and (vii) presenting a step-by-step guide on how to work with F-to-FCSA.

Structure of this book

Part I – The context

The first chapter provides the context of F-to-FCSA by investigating issues such as society's denial of FCSA and F-to-FCSA, the definitions and classifications of FCSA, the motivations behind it, its prevalence, both historical and more present, and the challenges around data collection, such as obtaining the correct data.

The second chapter accentuates the impact that patriarchal society and misogyny have had on the character formation of passive females and how this is linked to FCSA. The question of why some women sexually abuse children is scrutinised from several viewpoints. This chapter investigates some feminist authors' perspectives and explores their framing of this phenomenon. It then focusses on several psychodynamic authors' understandings and theories of masochism, perversion, and the stance of positioning a child as an extension of her mother's body. This chapter attempts not to leave any stone unturned in its pursuit of answering my original question: why do some women end up sexually abusing their children?

The third chapter consists of a case study of my client. It depicts a clear picture of the entrapment experience by a woman who was once a victim herself and who then became a child sexual perpetrator. Before her death and during her therapy, she made vast efforts to reach an inner resolution, including a confession.

Part II – Clinical implications

This part is divided into three sections: Between Scylla and Charybdis, Horror and sorrow – requires compassion and understanding, and Way forward.

The first section, Between Scylla and Charybdis, consists of three chapters: Ruth struggles with the Five-Headed Monster: the relational splits, The breaking and making boundaries=the whirlpool feels like enmeshment, and Working process and progress=between the devil and the deep blue sea.

In these chapters, an intimate narrative is portrayed of how Ruth, one of the interviewed therapists, processes her internal turmoil evoked by her client, who had sexually abused little girls and boys. The polar dynamics emanating from Ruth, the private person, who needs her womanhood protected, and Ruth, the professional, who must contain the extreme complexities and splits on the ward, are explored.

The second section, Horror and sorrow: requires compassion and understanding, is divided into three chapters: We see? Do we hear?, The mind-blowing venom of the FCSA, and Many faces, many levels. They speak of the personal narratives of Helen, Linda, Sarah, Greta, and Mary. These five female F-to-FCSA therapists all emphasise the need for therapists working with survivors and perpetrators of F-to-FCSA to hear the 'what': knowing and acknowledging what brought their client to this distressed situation before they can work with the 'how'; processing difficult content, feelings, thoughts, and behaviours. Furthermore, the need to develop a gender-perspective approach is stressed.

The third section, Way forward, consists of two chapters, Bold empathy and Conclusions and recommendations: guidance for clinicians. Bold empathy describes how the central requisites of boundaries and empathy cannot function in isolation from the other and must work in collaboration. The concept of Bold Empathy is founded on the overriding premise that asserts the direct impact that hearing and listening to the clients' past has on the therapeutic relationship, hence necessitating the need to enforce one's boundaries while still retaining empathy, compassion, and the capacity to bear what the client describes. Furthermore, the boldness refers to the need for the therapist to allow themselves to imagine the experience of enduring extremely disturbing trauma, expressed by either the victim or the perpetrator of sexual abuse. As far as I know, the concept of 'Bold Empathy' has not been used in the existing psychotherapy literature.

The last chapter of this book, Conclusions and recommendations: guidance for Clinicians, puts forth specific guidance on the application of Bold Empathy for therapists, supervisors, and researchers working with F-to-FCSA. The main purpose of this book is to equip clinicians by facilitating a more robust understanding and capacity to work therapeutically with the complex issues related to F-to-FCSA survivors and perpetrators. The recommendations in this chapter are derived from the analysed experiences of the therapists interviewed, as well as the childhood history and the therapeutic work experience of the author. They are intended to introduce releasing pathways that are functional for therapists, whilst generating meaningful transformation in the lives of F-to-FCSA survivors and perpetrators.

Confidentiality

The interviews produced extensive and granular analyses. It is important to note that to conceal personal details, all the therapists and their narratives have been anonymised, and all names have been invented. Although the verbatims are mainly original, they have also been changed to be more reader-friendly. The interviewed therapists gave their permission to have their narratives used for the PhD and any publication that follows, including a book. The same anonymising pertains to the case study or any references to client cases.

Conclusion

Therapeutic Work with Perpetrators and Survivors of Female-to-Female Child Sexual Abuse: A Clinician's Guide, in its complexity and darkness, was written with an overwhelming sense of hope (is a book of hope) in terms of providing further understanding for clinicians to be able to help survivors and perpetrators of F-to-FCSA process their multifaceted past and present experiences. The therapist uses her countertransference to reach her client by applying Bold Empathy, a decisive and concerted application of empathy and assertiveness, which allows her to imagine and feel what the client might be experiencing. The therapist commits to the therapeutic relationship with the survivors and perpetrators, even during those moments in the clinical work when optimism feels beyond one's grasp and the horizon of change is barely visible.

It is my sincere hope that this book, through the investigations of the theories related to F-to-FCSA, the lived experiences of the interviewed therapists, and the analysis of their narratives, will not only help to answer some of the questions about the development of female sexual perversion but also contribute to the therapeutic work transpiring with survivors and perpetrators of F-to-FCSA.

Part I

The context

But blue
Was the bosom of the silence
Where I lay

Carried away
To the night
So stormy
To the mountains
And a house
Windows facing the North

There she laid me
Facing the North

Her cloak all over
Her blue cloak
All over me

I sang a song
A song of the unspoken years
Lost in the unknown

Who was crying?
Was it me?
Or the trees?

With the longing known
So great
Only by the ocean
Far out in the North

That moment
The sky
So dark
The clouds
Like the souls of the birds
Gone long ago

I was a young teen when I wrote the above poem. In retrospect, I realise that it would have been impossible for me then to have been able to fully grasp what I was conveying. The meaning of my poem was revealed to me several years later. This revelation was initiated when I began to explore my memories of the sexual abuse perpetrated on me as an eight-year-old child. My perpetrator existed in the form of a mother figure who came to care for my sisters and me after my mother had died.

The poem above speaks resoundingly to me of the confusion, desperation, loneliness, and isolation I was living in. Through my poem, I described my experience of dissociation, confusion, and not knowing what had happened to me while trying to cope with the aftermath of being sexually abused by a mother figure. I liken the abusive experience to nauseating enmeshment and death, which was perpetrated into my defenceless, embryonic mind, soul, and body. I had to traverse the ensuing struggle, forced on me as an infant, to have to bear and wage inside of myself, whilst feeling immobilised by an inviolable barrier of infinite silence and loneliness.

For many years, I struggled with a deficient range of relevant vocabulary to describe what happened to me. I had never heard anyone talking about such abuse until I found an article in a newspaper mentioning the book '*Mother, Madonna and Whore: The Idealization and Denigration of Motherhood*' by Estella Welldon (2004). I had finally found an empowering language through which I was able to decode and process what had been done to me, namely, my childhood experience was being validated, and it was through this process that my life started to transform.

Since Welldon's (2004) seminal work was published, many clinicians have further researched and written books and articles about FCSA, including in-depth analyses of research on the prevalence of FCSA, its definitions, and the societal barriers to recognising its existence. The therapeutic profession is not immune to the permeation of these societal barriers. During my more than 20 years of practising, I have often been met with surprised eyes and questions when talking about F-to-FCSA to my colleagues. Therefore, it is important to set a context for this complex phenomenon by briefly discussing the definitions and classifications of FCSA, its prevalence, whilst engaging with the societal impediments hindering its recognition, in order to effectuate transformative FCSA treatment. For the treatment of FCSA to be effective, clinicians must understand the complexities of the definitions of FCSA as well as engage with the difficulties in recognising its existence.

Definition of FCSA

Munro (2000: 4) describes FCSA as the 'one which has no name'. Survivors of FCSA may not often have any words to describe or label the abuse they experienced. The definition of FCSA, in this context, may be regarded as my attempt to name the 'one which has no name'.

Debatably, early authors and clinicians brought forward an assumption that for a woman to commit such an abusive act, she must be mentally unstable, and her victims cannot be normal. A mother who sexually abused her daughters was regarded as severely disturbed, possibly psychotic, and easily identified by her community as a madwoman. In contrast, the male perpetrator of incest was alleged to have merged well within his neighbourhood (Forward and Buck, 1988). Mothers who perpetrated incest were judged as suffering frequently from mental retardation and brain damage impacting their impulse control (Mathis,

1972). Historical precedents have demonstrated that the relegation of female sexual perpetrators, as being mad or bad, can engender the propensity to incite a witch-hunt culture where these women are considered separate from everyday society. The categorisation of women who sexually abuse children must go beyond that dichotomy to enable clinicians to better understand the hidden layers of this complex abuse and recognise that women who sexually abuse children exist among us.

It is pivotal to note that the definitions explored in this chapter define mother-child sexual abuse (MCSA) and FCSA, not specifically F-to-FCSA, as I have not found a specific definition for F-to-FCSA. The task of defining FCSA is a complex yet essential process; moreover, while it can feel rigid and limiting, the examination itself can ultimately deconstruct and challenge our assumptions whilst broadening our understanding of FCSA, thus aiding practitioners and the public.

Reports of abuse perpetrated by females are often more susceptible to inquiries about their validity than reports of abuse perpetrated by males (Rosencrans, 1997). Establishing a standardised and universal clear-cut definition of FCSA is difficult due to the cultural variations as to what is regarded as the abusive and non-abusive treatment of children in different societies (Mitchell and Morse, 1998). To explore varying cultural determinants of what qualifies as abusive or non-abusive treatment of children extends the scope of this book. However, I would like to challenge the reductionist premise that not only asserts that CSA and FCSA are inherently cultural constructions, but that they can even be beneficial to the child. My challenge is rooted in the sacredness of the personal, namely, what child would willingly want to have such an experience, and what parent would want their child to be treated that way?

Many thoughts and questions about FCSA permeate both the professional and public domains. How can a woman perpetrate sexual abuse? Are the female perpetrators wicked, or do they express a misguided extension of motherly love? How can any evidence of FCSA be established when there is neither semen left by the perpetrator nor a feasible breakage of the hymen? It seems clear that FCSA sits at odds with a common perception that women cannot rape and penetrate.

The importance of the gender-specific definition

It is important to note that although Lombroso (1895) recognised by the late nineteenth century that women, whom he described as fairytale-like loathsome and horrendous figures, were capable of rape, present-day law in England and Wales does not acknowledge it due to their lack of a penis. Rape is defined as relating only to males and 'penile penetration' (Great Britain, Sexual Offences Act, 2003). Nonetheless, I am encouraged to see that the definition of HM Government of CSA (2023) considers women capable of rape and other child sexual offences.

Before defining FCSA specifically, it is necessary to highlight Rosencran's obvious points (1997: 20) regarding FCSA and hopefully establish clarity on stereotypical assumptions about FCS perpetrators.

1 'A woman does not have a penis'.
2 'A woman can be sexual without a penis'.
3 'Sexual abuse can occur without a penis'.
4 'To explore sexual abuse by women thoroughly means to explore outside the conventional concepts about women, mothers, sex, mother/child relationships, and heterosexuality'.
5 'The mother perpetrators may have been sexually abused by men and later recreated those abusive dynamics but with themselves as the abusers and their daughters as the victims'.

FCSA must be defined outside the framework of male-dominated definitions (Rosencrans, 1997), and aspects such as females having greater levels of intimacy with children than men must be considered (Saradjian, 1996).

Lawson (1993: 265, 266) defined MCSA of male children by dividing it into five categories: subtle, seductive, perverse, overt, and sadistic. Her definition of it, which I have adopted, will be used when defining not only maternal but also any FCSA. The five categories presented briefly are below:

- **Subtle abuse consists of** behaviors that may not intentionally be sexual in nature but serve to meet the parent's emotional and/or sexual needs at the expense of the child's emotional and/or developmental needs...
- **Seductive abuse implicates** 'sexual stimulation that is inappropriate for the child's age and/or is motivated by the parent's sexual needs'. It:

  ...implies conscious awareness and intention of arousing or stimulating the child sexually. Such behaviors may include exhibitionistic displays of nudity or sexual behavior; exposure to pornographic materials or exposure to seductive posing, gestures, or verbal messages. Seductive abuse is non-coercive and may be experienced as confusing, over-stimulating, or pleasurable by the child.

- **Perverse sexual abuse** involves 'behavior such as...criticizing the child's rate of sexual development, threatening the child with fear of homosexuality...'
- **Overt sexual abuse** includes 'attempted intercourse, cunnilingus, anilingus, fellatio, genital fondling, digital penetration...' and 'involves some form of coercion and/or threats to discourage disclosure'.
- **Sadistic sexual abuse** comprises maternal/female 'sexual behavior that is intended to hurt the child and may be part of a general pattern of severe physical and emotional abuse'.

Classifying FCSA

Classifying FCSA is complex and not straightforward, and it is presented here based on a more contemporary and broader stance.

McCarty (1986) studied 26 female sexual incest offenders and classified them, based on the nature of their offences, into three groups: independent offenders, co-offenders, and accomplices. The independent offender is characterised as having a traumatic childhood, being seriously emotionally disturbed, and regarding her daughter as an extension of herself. The co-offender is described as having borderline intelligence, actively taking part in the sexual abuse, and seeing herself as someone who needs more care than her victims. The accomplice who also regards her needs as more important than the victims may be aware of the sexual abuse and never do anything about it.

Mathews, Matthews, and Speltz (1994) divided female sexual offenders also into three different groups, which are briefly described here:

1 Predisposed Offenders are women who reported being sexually abused when young and often by family members. They offend alone and target very young children. Saradjian (1996) expounded that the women belonging to this group regard their victims as unwanted and very similar to themselves or their abuser/s and gain power and gratification through the abuse.
2 Teacher-lover offenders target adolescents whom they regard as similar to themselves or their idolised partners. The adolescent children are perceived as wanted by the female offenders, and the sexual act is to gain physical pleasure and control and construct a fantasy of being in a relationship with the adolescent child.
3 Male-coerced offenders are passive women who are initially coerced into offending by men. In this group, according to Saradjian (1996), the women see their victims as peers and as being like themselves. They also have fantasies regularly about the children, followed by masturbation. A study by Davin, Hislop, and Dunbar (1999) found that 75% of female co-offenders lived in a physically and psychologically violent and possessive relationship in which they became compliant partners forced to perform unusual sex acts to satisfy their partner's demands.

Saradjian (1996) established another category, an atypical female perpetrator, who does not fit into the previous categories. An atypical perpetrator may abuse a child as an equal partner with men, and/or coerce a man to sexually abuse a child. She might also sexually abuse a child while in a dissociative state or when experiencing psychosis.

Ritual abuse is a qualitatively different category from other sexual abuse (Scott, 2001). It is associated with religious and supernatural repetitive activities that purposefully frighten the child (Finkelhor et al., 1988). Women perform gendered roles in ritually abusive families, such as cleaning up, comforting, silencing the victims, and preparing the daughters for involvement in pornography, prostitution, and ritual abuse. Some women reserve their daughters for sexual/reproductive access by specifically chosen men (Scott, 2001).

Motivations behind female child sexual abuse

Female perversion serves as a mask that conceals underlying emptiness and depression. For some women, this perversion, manifested through fantasies and acting out, becomes a central preoccupation in their lives and may serve as a source of comfort and control. The emptiness these women experience often extends to their relational areas (Motz, 2008). Many female sexual perpetrators have poor or nearly non-existent relationships with their partners and other social groups, leading them to feel that the abusive relationship fulfils their needs for control, emotional bonding, and support (Ford, 2006). Motherhood may also evolve into a medium for expressing rage and influence (Motz, 2008).

The statistics seem to suggest that most female sexual perpetrators do not have a sexual motivation for their actions (Ford, 2006; O'Connor, 1987). Nevertheless, some of the women reported arousal when fantasising sexually about their victims, although the arousal was more correlated to the feelings of control during the abuse (Ford, 2006). It should be borne in mind that some perpetrators do not report their sexual fantasies about children out of shame and fear.

The prevalence of FCSA

The historical evidence

What does a historical reading tell us about known cases of FCSA? As can be seen from Lombroso's historical account of child abuse by women in the nineteenth century, the absent/dead mother and evil stepmother were not just a fantasy. Many mothers died in childbirth, and, for example, in the seventeenth and eighteenth centuries, 80% of widowers remarried within a year of their wife's death. Offspring faced the antagonism of new stepmothers and their children. Wet nurses also had a vital part in the mothering of the children because, until the mid-nineteenth century, it was common to idealise wet nurses despite the high mortality rate and abuse of the children (Lombroso, 1895).

Lombroso examined the physical, mental, and pathological characteristics of female offenders. His book echoes a horror story in which the skulls, brains, fingers, and jaws of female offenders were measured. He describes all the female offenders as ugly and horrible-looking, although their actual published pictures seem to portray normal-looking women. He claimed that the offending women were not uglier than the male criminals, while he argued, by quoting Rykere, that 'Feminine criminality…is more cynical, more depraved, and more terrible than the criminality of the male', and, quoting Corraro Celto, that 'their perversity of mind is more fertile in new crimes than the imagination of a judge in new punishment' (Lombroso, 1895: 147).

Lombroso described numerous cases of women who committed various crimes, including infanticide, and rape. He explained the difference between a 'normal' woman and a female sexual perpetrator as:

> …a normal woman will refuse herself to her lover rather than injure her child; but the female criminal is different. *She* will prostitute her daughter to preserve her paramour.

(Lombroso, 1895: 153–154)

Chapter 1

Can anyone see? Can anyone hear?

Introduction

Untitled poem (Lea Getu, 1974, cited in Motz, 2020)

It was a dying night
I lay in my bed
And waited
Silently waited

Not a step I heard
No voices
When silence entered my room

Did I hear?
Did I tremble?

Still I lay
I lay
All alone

A blue cloak she had
The silence
To hide me in
And carry away
Like one carries a child

Did anyone hear?
Do our hearts remember?

No storm was there that night
Just a moon
Far in a distance
So red

DOI: 10.4324/9781003607007-3

Although I was surprised to find Lombroso openly writing as early as 1895 about female rapists and women who kill and prostitute their children, his statements fit the fantasy prototype of seeing offending females as ugly and exceptionally evil.

There are even earlier descriptions of women collectively partaking in the sexual abuse of a child. De Mause (1976) refers to the words of Petronius (ca. 27–66 AD) who describes groups of women clapping their hands around a bed where a young girl is being raped. Saradjian (2010) depicts many historical instances of females sexually abusing children. She refers, e.g., to Tardieu (1857), who acknowledged that the sexual perpetrators were mainly men, while some women likewise committed such criminalities, and to Bernard (1886), who maintained that in France, between 1874 and 1884, 181 women were sentenced for perpetrating child sexual abuse. However, after all this evidence, to use the words by Freund and his colleagues as late as 1984, 'pedophilia…does not exist at all in women' (in Saradjian, 2010: 10) is unfathomable.

The difficulties in getting the correct data on the prevalence

Understandably, data on the prevalence of FCSA depends on recognition of FCSA and its reporting. This problem was recognised by Gibb (1894, in Saradjian, 2010), the Examining Physician to the New York Society for Prevention of Cruelty to Children who asserted that the number of reported victims of FCSA does not correlate with the actual number of incidences.

I believe that the true extent of FCSA remains unknown. Any available data is a by-product of general sexual abuse studies, and any estimates should be regarded as tentative. One might say this is a widespread and chronic problem concerning CSA and FCSA historically.

Various research findings report a disparity in the data of FCSA depending on how the abuse by female perpetrators is defined and the methodology used for its analysis. Finkelhor and Russell (1984) compared the data analysis of the American Humane Association and the National Center on Child Abuse and Neglect (1981) and found that the difference in their respective findings was due to the variances in defining FCSA; if the definition was kept within the category of females acting alone, the number of female victims increased.

Without any hesitation, there are many disparities regarding the prevalence of FCSA. What we also know is that most of the sexual crimes against children are committed by men, as it is estimated that 97%–98% of sex offenders are men (Finkelhor, 1986; Mrazek et al., 1981). Therefore, we may assume that the remaining 2%–3% of offenders are women. But in reality, the number is unknown, and the conclusion is that it is highly probable that there may still be a significant number of females who sexually abuse children.

Presentation of some more recent prevalence studies

The data presented above is 20–40 years old. I have therefore investigated some more contemporary research findings as to the prevalence of female child sexual offences, which reveal that the reporting of FCSA has greatly increased in the past 15 years. However, finding data that discloses the extent of offending by female perpetrators and their female victims remains difficult.

I contacted the Home Office in 2009 to enquire as to why there was no collected data on female offenders and the gender of their victims. I got an email that explained that the Home Office has no responsibility to collect crime statistics recorded by the police, and no information is held on the alleged offenders. There is no requirement for the police to notify the Home Office of any offender details. This has been the case since crime data was first collected in 1857. In addition, they informed me that the data collected by the Ministry of Justice (MoJ), which used to be part of the Home Office, contains information on gender, age, and offences of perpetrators who go through the courts, prisons, and probation services. Could it be time to instigate some changes to the 1857 laws on how data is collected on sex offenders and to introduce a provision that includes the records of both the offender's and the victim's gender and age?

While the prevalence of FCSA remains low, the National Society for the Prevention of Cruelty to Children (NSPCC) Child Protection argues that its prevalence may be higher than official figures suggest. According to NSPCC, up to 5% of child sexual offences are perpetrated by females, and often, very young children are sexually abused by their caregivers more frequently than older children (Community Care, 2005).

Whilst the previous study rather tentatively suggested that the official figures of FCSA are higher than the existing data, the research from Lucy Faithful Foundation (LFF) estimates that there could be as many as 64,000 female child sex offenders in Britain and that sexual abuse by females is much more extensive than previously comprehended results indicating that FCSA is 'up to 20% of a conservative estimate of 320,000 suspected UK paedophiles were women' (Townsend and Syal, 2009). The LFF data is correlated with findings by the NSPCC, which demonstrates that between 2004 and 2009, the number of children phoning Childline, reporting being sexually abused by a female, increased by 132% (Darling, 2017).

The Crime Survey for England and Wales (CSEW) (2023) statistics ending March 2019 estimated that out of 1,647 (unweighted base – number of adult) women who were sexually abused before the age of 16, 3.4% had experienced sexual abuse by both male and female, while a further 1.5% experienced sexual abuse by female only. It is estimated that out of the 1,487 female victims, 1.6% were sexually abused by their mother and 0.4% by their stepmother. What is lacking in this data is the gender of the other perpetrators, such as carers, friends, and relatives. Out of 485 females (unweighted base – number of adults), 1.4% had been raped by or assaulted by penetration (including attempts) by female and 2.5% by both female and male. In addition to the statistic being interesting on its own, it has another relevant point – it classifies women as being capable of rape and that women can be raped and penetrated by females.

Getting correct data on FCSA, in general, is problematic, as many survivors do not report their trauma or do not know that what happened to them was sexual abuse. Some victims also do not remember the perpetrator or do not want to disclose who sexually abused them (CSEW, 2023). The number of articles on FCSA has increased in the media, and hopefully, that will expand the reporting and more accurate data collection.

In short, I investigated the complexity involved in defining and categorising female sexual abuse and offered various gender-specific definitions of FCSA whilst exploring their utility for clinicians. I subsequently examined the historical evidence of FCSA and investigated the persisting structural challenges around the obtainment of reliable data that would accurately reflect the occurrence of FCSA. I concluded by presenting the limited historical and contemporary data relating to the prevalence of FCSA, as well as offering a brief critique of current data collection systems.

Bibliography

Community Care (2005) NSPCC warns women abusers may slip through the net. Community Care, 16 November 2005. Available at: https://www.communitycare.co.uk/2005/11/16/nspcc-warns-women-abusers-may-slip-through-the-net/ (Accessed: 10 May 2025).

Crime Survey for England and Wales (2023) Available at: https://www.ons.gov.uk/people-populationandcommunity/crimeandjustice/datasets/sexualoffendingcrimesurveyforeng-landandwalesappendixtables (Accessed: 28 February 2025).

Darling, A. (2017) The truth about female sex offenders. The Telegraph, 07 March 2017. Retrieved 13/05/2025 from World Wide Web: https://www.telegraph.co.uk/women/life/truth-female-sex-offenders/

Davin, P., Hislop, J. and Dunbar, T. (1999) Female Sexual Abusers: Three Views. Brandon: Safer Society Press.

de Mause, L. (ed.) (1976) The History of Childhood: The Evolution of Parent-Child Relationships as a Factor in History. London: Souvenir Press.

Finkelhor, D. and Russell, D.E. (1984) Child Sexual Abuse: New Theory and Research. New York: The Free Press.

Finkelhor, D. (1986). A sourcebook on child sexual abuse. California: Sage Publications.

Finkelhor, D., Williams, L. and Burns, N. (1988) Nursery Crimes: Sexual Abuse in Day Care. Newbury Park, CA: Sage Publications.

Ford, H. (2006) Women Who Sexually Abuse Children. Chichester: John Wiley& Sons, Ltd.

Forward, S. and Buck, C. (1988) Betrayal of Innocence: Incest and Its Devastation. Revised ed. New York: Penguin Books.

Great Britain Sexual Offences Act (2003) Available at: https://www.legislation.gov.uk/ukpga/2003/42/contents (Accessed: 08 December 2024).

Lawson, C. (1993) Mother-son sexual abuse: Rare or underreported?: A critique of the research. Child Abuse and Neglect, 17(2), 261–269.

Lombroso, C. (1895) The Female Offender. New York: D. Appleton and Company.

Mathews, R., Matthews, J. and Speltz, K. (1994) Female sexual Offenders: An Exploratory Study. Orwell: Safer Society.

Mathis, J. (1972) Clear Thinking about Sexual Deviations. Chicago, IL: Nelson-Hall Company.

McCarty, L. (1986) Mother-child incest: Characteristics of the offender. Child Welfare, 65(5), pp. 447–458.

Mitchell, J. and Morse, J. (1998) *From Victims to Survivors: Reclaimed Voices of Women Sexually Abused in Childhood by Females.* Washington, DC: Accelerated Development.

Mish, F (ed.) (1983) *Webster's Ninth New Collegiate Dictionary.* Spring Field: Merriam-Webster Inc.

Motz, A. (2008) *The Psychology of Female Violence; Crimes against the Body.* 2nd ed. London: Routledge.

Motz, A. (2020) 'Taboo: Female psychopathy and sexual offending against children', in Motz, A., Dennis, M. and Aiyegbusi, A. (eds.) *Invisible Trauma: Women, Difference and the Criminal System.* London: Routledge, pp. 100–116.

Mrazek, P., Lynch, M. and Bentovim, A. (1981) 'Recognition of child sexual abuse in the United Kingdom', in Mrazek, P. and Kempe, H. (eds.) *Sexually Abused Children and Their Families.* New York: Pergamon Press, pp. 35–50.

Munro, K. (2000) Mother-daughter sexual abuse: A painful topic. Available at: https://kalimunro.com/articles-info/sexual-emotional-abuse/mother-daughter-sexual-abuse/ (Accessed: 08 December 2024).

O'Connor, A. (1987) Female sex offenders. *British Journal of Psychiatry*, 150(5), pp. 615–620. https://doi.org/10.1192/bjp.150.5.615

Rosencrans, B. (1997) *The Last Secret: Daughters Sexually Abused by Mothers.* Brandon: Safer Society Press.

Saradjian, J. (1996) *Women Who Sexually Abuse Children: From Research to Clinical Practice.* Chichester: John Wiley & Sons.

Saradjian, J. (2010) 'Understanding the prevalence of female-perpetrated sexual abuse and the impact of that abuse on victims', in Gannon, A. and Corton, F. (eds.) *Female Sexual Offenders: Theory, Assessment and Treatment.* Chichester: Wiley-Blackwell, pp. 9–30.

Scott, S. (2001) *The Politics and Experience of Ritual Abuse Beyond Disbelief.* Buckingham: Open University Press.

Townsend, M. and Syal, R. (2009) Up to 64,000 women in UK 'are child-sex offenders'. *The Guardian*, 4 October 2009. https://www.theguardian.com/society/2009/oct/04/uk-female-child-sex-offenders (Accessed 10 May 2025).

Welldon, E. ([1988] 2004) *Mother, Madonna and Whore: The Idealization and Denigration of Motherhood.* London: Karnac.

Chapter 2

An exploration of why some women sexually abuse children

Introduction

At first, it is critical to specify that almost all women who have suffered various traumas never become sexual abusers. When exploring theories and their links with FCSA, my probe is positioned from the bottom up: from the individual history and experience of the offending women, and not from the top down, the general female population. The theories presented are not used for pathologising and labelling any women, including survivors and perpetrators. Also, not all offenders fit into all the proposed theories, although many do, as the research shows.

This chapter explores society's construction of women as passive and incapable of abusing children by examining writings by some well-known feminists and their views on FCSA. Some existing data and links between FCSA and patriarchal society are considered. A definition of masochism is offered, followed by a critical examination of early psychoanalytic developments and female depictions. Benjamin's (1986) intersubjective view of masochism and the difficulty for a daughter to identify with her desexualised and submissive mother are investigated. The links between masochism and FCSA are explored, and how the offending woman fails to separate from her mother whilst being enmeshed with her daughter. Stoller's (1986) understanding of perversion as a form of erotic hatred, as well as examining Glenn's (1984) notion of mastering trauma through masochism, are probed and linked to FCSA. Welldon's (2004) understanding of narcissistic mothers, the symbiotic relationship between the perverse mother and her daughter, and the notion of transgenerational trauma are investigated and linked to FCSA. In addition, 'Glasser's (2003) core complex' and the psychodynamic understanding of the embodied nature of perverse motherhood are considered. The childhood histories of both female sexual perpetrators and victims are explored to uncover supporting links of the perpetrated sexual abuse to the perpetrators' trauma histories.

Patriarchal society and its links to FCSA

In traditional feminist thinking, men, in general, are regarded as the abusers and sexual aggressors, whilst females are predominantly regarded as the victims. Females, from an early age, had to learn to submit to men's dominance due to their economic

DOI: 10.4324/9781003607007-4

dependency and lack of social and political power. Men were viewed as having been socialised to believe that it is first and foremost females who must fulfil their needs, and women became regarded as sexual commodities. So, customarily, it is the patriarchy that is observed as giving ground, opportunity, and motivation for males to abuse children (Seymour, 1998). But what about the female perpetrators, and what are the links established between patriarchal society and FCSA?

A straightforward answer would be that the powerless victimised woman within the domain of the patriarchal society may develop a masochistic personality, identify with the male aggressor, and become the abuser of vulnerable children within the private sphere of the home and other caring institutions. But is this the answer? Have we now solved the link between patriarchal society and FCSA?

FCSA has been largely minimised or denied by feminist authors whose focus has been mainly on the sexual violence committed by men (Fitzroy, 1999). It was taken for granted until the late 1990s that all sexual abusers were male. In general, feminist thinkers seem to argue that it is a patriarchal society and the oppression of women that lies behind women's abusive behaviour (Young, 1994).

The feminist theory of patriarchy, if taken as the only reason for sexual violence towards children, hinders us from recognising women's sexually abusive behaviour towards children in general. The position that all sexual perpetrators are men seems to support the feminist theory about male power and that abuse is one of the means to oppress women in a patriarchal society (Young, 1994). In that context, the possibility that females are potential perpetrators could be perceived as undermining feminist theories. While men commit most sexual crimes and most of their victims are women, it remains imperative that any existing research links between male violence and FCSA are explored.

In my MA research (Getu, 2003), I explored the phenomena of F-to-FCSA, and one of my research questions attempted to illustrate the links between misogyny and FCSA. I found that eight respondents who had been sexually abused by their mothers and/or other females described their grandfathers as absent, abusive, and misogynistic, and their fathers as absent and/or weak. In their words: 'maternal and paternal grandparents were unknown'; 'granddad was an alcoholic'; '…infectious'; 'abusive patriarch'; 'a violent man at times and I think intimidated at the very least my grandmother'; 'very rigid, cruel man'; 'my maternal grandfather died when I was two'. Of their grandmothers, respondents said, '…suffered from depression'; '… died before I was born. I was told my grandfather used to beat her'. The same respondents described their fathers as 'I never knew him'; 'killed before I was born'; 'left when I was about four…a passive, weak individual…I learned as he was dying that his mother had abused him…I never really felt accepted by him… never felt I had a father'; 'he was unavailable when at home'; 'my mother has been married five times'.

Whilst my MA research recognised that female sex offenders had abusive or absent grandfathers and fathers, the findings presented by Petrovich and Templar (1984) of a self-report study established that from the sample group of 83 prisoners convicted of rape, 59% had been molested by a female in their childhood.

In 56 cases, the sexual abuse had happened more than once, and 12 of them had been molested by more than one female. The average age of the boys was 10.81 years at the time of the molestation, and 82% of cases involved intercourse. Unfortunately, as the study was not their research, it lacks references to the original resources.

A similar report on serial rapists by Burgess and Hazelwood (1987) showed that out of their sample group of 41 male rapists, 56% had been sexually abused as a child. Of their perpetrators, 40% were women. Groth and Birnbaum (1979) studied 500 identified offenders through institutional and communal programmes. The findings were based on interviews with the offenders and some of their victims. The analysis established that about one-third of the men had experienced sexual trauma as a child. 27% of their perpetrators were adult females, and 14% were female peers. Most of the victims were sexually abused within an incestuous context.

While these older significant studies found that several male sexual perpetrators had been abused by females and contradicted the claim that only males are aggressors and females are victims, more research needs to be done on what proportion of male sexual offenders have been sexually abused by females. Arguably, previous studies demonstrate that male sexual violence seems to be, to some extent, intertwined with female sexual violence. They also bring empirical evidence to the theory of identification with the aggressor, investigated later in this chapter.

Some changes have been undertaken regarding the understanding of FCSA. In the early 1990s, traditional feminist views that regarded female abusers as non-existent began to be challenged. Feminists had to take a new look at CSA and start exploring why some women, both heterosexual and lesbian, abuse each other and children sexually. The issue of CSA became less political and involved more personal complexity (Warner, 2009).

For Fitzroy (1999), feminism offers tools to understand FCSA. She developed a theoretical framework that examines the links between female sexual violence and patriarchal society. Her viewpoint incorporates aspects of feminism and post-modern theory, especially regarding the construction of gender and power relations. Fitzroy tentatively suggests that female sexual offenders are a direct outcome of systemic structures of hierarchy and misogyny, whereby the identities of women, men, and children are assembled. Her argument extends further, asserting that women's sexually offending behaviour is a direct manifestation of society's construction of 'mothering' and the 'other'. It is within a fundamentally patriarchal historical and social context that women learn to categorise, oppress, and dehumanise those whom they perceive as being in an inferior position. Fitzroy (1999) refers to Welldon's (2004) and Saradjian's (1996) writings on the abusive mother internalising her own abusive experience; collectively, their work brings a more profound focus on the misogyny constructed by society, demonstrating that the mother is internalising much more than solely her own experience of CSA. Therefore, the mother learns to hate and despise her own body and directs her rage towards the substitute self-object, her daughter's body, which she may regard as an extension of herself. Fitzroy's previous viewpoint relates to the notion of 'identification with the aggressor' (Freud, 1993).

While Fitzroy (1999) seems to support general feminist theories about 'patriarchal' society as a cause of women's violent sexual behaviour, she also recognises women's capacity to be abusive towards their children. Specifically, a female victim of CSA might repeat her experienced sexual trauma as an attempt to create a sense of adult identity whilst also exercising dominance over the other – the child. One could claim that post-modernism challenges the traditional dichotomous idea that masculinity is inherently aggressive, whilst femininity automatically connotes passiveness. Instead, women's position should not be viewed as either baddie or victim but as fluid, dynamic, and paradoxical, and existing within numerous discourses.

Considering masculinity and femininity as cultural and historical constructions within which the individual tries to find a place, and by using structural analysis of society, one can examine the socially legitimated power relations, including women's use and access to violence (Koonin, 1995). Linking sexual violence entirely to a homogeneously aggressive masculinity attributes to society's failure to see the possibility of women being sexually violent towards their children. By imagining that women abuse solely in conjunction with men, we limit women's capability to change, comprehend, and draw their own conclusions, and we essentially disregard women's potential. To believe in women's innocence and capability to initiate sexual violence only when sexualised and groomed by a man is sexist, and not feminist (Young, 1994).

If we are to accept power dynamics within patriarchy, both historical and social in scope, we must accept that women cannot be exempt from the evolution of their own power dynamics resulting from fluctuating power positions or an endemic vulnerability; women, too, can assume roles where power is exercised or abused. And motherhood might present a chance for women to act out a desire for control.

Welldon (2004) describes a social situation in which a mother who has been a victim of male violence feels powerless and isolated. She identifies with her male aggressor and acts out her violence against her child, who, in turn, becomes the helpless victim. In her words, she describes perversion being:

> intertwined with the politics of power; one aspect is psychological and the other social. It is possible that this difference of response is caused by society's inability to see woman as a complete human being. The difficulties in acknowledging that mothers can abuse their power could be the result of total denial, as a way of dealing with this unpalatable truth. Woman is seen as a part-object, a mere receptacle for man's perverse designs.
>
> (Welldon, 2004: 104, 105)

In the context of previous discussions regarding women as not just passive but as fluid, dynamic, and full of potential, the claim that women are powerless victims who have no choices seems implausible. One should not excuse adult women's violent behaviour and view women as incapable of making choices and being responsible for their crimes, including sexual violence perpetrated against children.

The survivors of FCSA inform us that women can actively enact sexual violence towards children. Though many women are initially coerced by men to sexually abuse children and participate in it under male control, some women coerce men to harm the child as an equal partner with the man, and/or abuse the child alone.

Internalised misogyny, together with experienced childhood trauma, may provide a framework for why women abuse children sexually. However, it is not the only reason for women to be sexually abusive towards children.

The passive and masochistic female

While the existing links between socially constructed and internalised misogyny and FCSA provide useful information, it is necessary to examine in greater detail the reasons given as to why some women sexually abuse children. Therefore, the understanding of the development of a woman who has grown up under such misogynist constructions and has been moulded into their constructions is crucial. I shall call that woman a passive and masochistic female – yet I ask whether such a female is truly passive and masochistic, and how this notion is linked to FCSA.

The word 'masochism' was created by sexologist Richard von Krafft-Ebing after Leopold von Sacher-Masoch (1870), who depicted in his book 'Venus in Furs', a world filled with rules, whips, and suspense. Masochism, according to Merriam-Webster, is defined as 'a sexual perversion characterized by pleasure in being subjected to pain or humiliation [...] pleasure in being abused or dominated: a taste for suffering...' (Mish, 1983: 730).

Some early views of a masochistic female

In the history of psychoanalysis, femininity was traditionally described as being characterised by passivity. Freud (1961: 6) claimed that masochism is 'an expression of feminine nature' which is 'most accessible to our observation...'. He based his notion of female masochism on the theories of penis envy and the feminine Oedipus complex. His ideas were supported by several authors, e.g., Bonaparte (1953) and Deutsch (1945), who maintained that female masochism is a crucial aspect of a woman's sexual and psychic life.

Stoller (1986: 27, 28) critically quotes Freud's viewpoints of women as follows: 'women are secretive and insincere'; 'more masochistic'; 'less self-sufficient'; 'more dependent and pliant'; 'more envious and jealous'; 'have defective super-egos'; '...little sense of justice'; 'weaker in social interests'; 'have less capacity for sublimating instincts'; 'and become more rigid and unchangeable at an earlier age'. All these quotes describe women as inferior and born with defects, both intellectually and emotionally.

Arkin (1984 in Allen, 1991) critically maintained that Freud viewed women as passive and men as the active aggressors, not just as everyday phenomena but also within the complexes of incest and that Freud's hypothesis on the taboo surrounding incest stems from the conflict of the male members of the family competing for the sexual services of the passive females.

It is important to note that Freud himself had a patient, 'Wolfman', who had vivid memories of his sister sexually abusing him (Freud, 2001). 'Dora', another one of Freud's patients, had a relationship with the powerful, seductive female Frau K., which is characterised by Scharff and Scharff (1994: 155) as follows:

> With Frau K. she is subject to the intimacies of sexual interest and failure, to sexual arousal as they read sexual books together, and to the homosexual stimulation of sleeping with a beautiful, sexually arousing young woman during Dora's period of adolescent sexual awakening.

They assert that Freud, through his theories based on his sexual drive analysis, failed to recognise the seductive dynamics brought to Dora's sexually developing life by Mr. K, Mrs. K, and Dora's parents.

While it is widely debated that Freud (1989) regarded women as passive masochists and on the receiving end of sexual experiences, he also acknowledged mothers as active and very powerfully affecting their children's sexual development. He argued:

> the seducer is regularly the mother…, for it was really the mother who by her activities over the child's bodily hygiene inevitably stimulated, and perhaps even roused for the first time, pleasurable sensations in her genitals.
>
> (Freud, 1989: 149, 150)

There seems to exist a contradiction related to female masochism in that the masochist desires to be dominated and lose her agency, whilst her search for being dominated is full of domination and active agency. Psychoanalyst Theodor Reik (1957) asserted that the masochist's need and ability to control through his cloak of duplicity enables a spectrum of oppositional behaviours and characteristics to manifest in disguise.

As psychoanalytic theory developed, men continued to be regarded as ruthlessly sexually aggressive, while women were regarded as submissive receivers. For example, Mathis (1972: 54) contended that women are sexually harmless due to not having a penis. He also argued that societies do not fully accept that women have sexual agency and active sexual drives and maintained that civilisation 'never becomes very excited' about the minor incidents of FCSA. Another analyst, West, wrote as late as 1987 that 'sexual deviations are much commoner in men than in women, arguably because men are more imaginative and venturesome!' (cited in Allen, 1991: 13). Both authors denied women as active sexual beings and described sexual deviations as exciting, full of imagination, and something the person chooses to have.

If we take Merriam-Webster's (Mish, 1983) definition of masochism at face value and regard women as masochistic and seeking to be sexually dominated and humiliated, it necessitates questioning how such a passive and masochistic creature can actively sexually abuse children. How could a docile woman, and especially a mother, far from being a monster and a 'purer' form of womanhood, be responsible for CSA?

Benjamin's intersubjective view of a passive female

An exploration of the links between FCSA and the further psychoanalytic understanding of female masochism can shed some light on women who abuse children sexually. It is important to keep in mind that most of the women, including those who had absent fathers or neglecting/abusive fathers, never become child sex perpetrators.

The perspectives by psychoanalyst and inter-subjectivist Benjamin (1986), on the development of female masochism, explain how mother-daughter relationships, together with an absent father figure, may contribute to the development of a masochistic female and how that may expand to evolve into the development of an abusive female.

Benjamin defines masochism as: 'The perversion of woman's sexual agency, the alienation of desire...' (Benjamin, 1986: 119) and argues that there is a growing understanding that girls achieve their gender identity by identifying with their mother's maternal attributes. She describes an ideal mother-daughter relationship in which the baby's sense of self is developed as a direct result of her mother's validation and acknowledgement of her existence.

Yet, from the vantage point of the daughter, a mother is not seen as a sexual subject, not a woman with active desire, but someone who serves only her child's interests. The mother presents herself as someone who has no control over her destiny, nor freedom to fulfil her own will, while her submission conforms to the perception that there is something inherently missing in women, which can only be made complete by men. A woman, who experiences herself as passive, feels that it is only through a masculine orientation and its represented potency and activity that she can derive her sexual agency from. The daughter of the passive mother cannot identify with her desexualised mother and base her representation of active desire on her; instead, she wishes to turn to her father, her representation of desire and active love (Benjamin, 1986).

Benjamin puts forward the argument that female desire is tied up with the fantasy of submission to the ideal archetypal male and inherently in conflict with her sense of agency. These contradictory forces manifest as masochism and function as a detached endeavour to resolve this internal conflict. 'The search for ideal love, the erotization of submission in fantasy or reality, points us back to the problem of masochism' and how it is an alienated attempt to resolve the problem of female desire, which is functioning as a detached attempt to resolve this internal conflict (Benjamin, 1986: 114).

According to Benjamin (1986), the challenges in the representation stem from the dissonance between the identification and separation from a desexualised mother and the inability to identify with an idealised father. She argues that the propensity for female masochism can be located within the specificity of gender identification and separation-individuation that result from female parenting. The frustration in girls during the phase of separation-individuation leads them to seek ideal love and become submissive. The father's power and his desired phallus stand for difference and separation from the mother for both sexes (Benjamin, 1986).

Benjamin (1986) refers to Mahler's (1956) notion of the rapprochement process as a period when the child's awareness of her independence and separation intensifies, while she wishes to gain back her dependency on her primary parent. The child paradoxically wishes to be recognised as independent by the primary parent on whom she also wants to depend. The child gains a consciousness of will and agency through this process of wanting to be recognised. In other words, the child becomes a subject of desire while also wanting to be recognised as an object.

This rapprochement period coincides with the development of the child's gender identity. The girls, unlike boys, find it difficult to separate from an attachment to their mothers. The girl needs another object, something which is not her own, to represent her desire. She idealises her father who represents her freedom, separation, and desire and identifies with her father's symbol of the phallus making her desire to incorporate her father sexually while wanting to be recognised by him (Benjamin, 1986).

The failure of the father to recognise his daughter's need for him to be offered as an object of identification may cause difficulties in integrating the development of the girl's independence, self-esteem, and sense of agency. Benjamin's (1986) conclusion is that the complex repercussions resulting from either a failing paternal identification or its full absence, constitute the blueprint for a perverse ideal of love, making women become drawn to relationships of submission due to an inherent need to find an ideal love and to reconstitute the ideal father-daughter relationship in which their desire and subjectivity will be recognised. The woman wishes to recognise herself in the idealised other and resolve her experienced conflict between activity and passivity.

Olivier (1989) also describes a little girl's development in similar terms to Benjamin; the little girl is not being desired by her mother while seeking to identify with her idealised and often absent father object. In the absence of the idealised male, the young daughter cannot differentiate from her mother and finds establishing her own identity and agency complicated and disturbed. She becomes traumatised and develops a masochistic character in an attempt to find the absent ideal male to identify with. Although both Olivier's (1989) and Benjamin's (1986) hypotheses tell us how the absence of an idealised male seems to play its part in the development of female masochism, her theory does not give us answers regarding what the effects on the little girl would be if her mother did not allow her daughter to separate from her.

Various studies support Benjamin's view about the little girl becoming traumatised due to an absent father figure. Cavanagh Johnson (1989) studied 13 girls between the ages of four and 12 who were attending a treatment programme due to their serious sexually abusive behaviour towards other children. The study found that most girls did not know where their fathers were. Five of the fathers had molested their children, and one father had molested his daughter with his wife. One of the fathers had left the daughter's mother, who was at the time abusing her daughter. Five of the fathers never lived with their daughters for any significant period. Just one father attended the treatment sessions with the girl's mother, only to be found out that he was molesting her daughter. All the natural fathers were abusive in various ways and could not hold down a job.

Although a link between masochism and patriarchal society, between the submissive mother and absent but potent and frustrating father has been investigated, the question remains: How is masochism/perversion linked to FCSA specifically if the FCSA perpetrator does not seem outwardly, in her perverse behaviour, to seek either any ideal man or punish her mother/herself for not letting her separate? Arguably, e.g., the adult women depicted in the cases of 'Wolfman' and 'Dora' could not be regarded traditionally as passive masochists who desire to be humiliated and dominated by another human being without taking an active role in sexual seductions. Therefore, further links of female masochism and its links with FCSA need to be considered.

Further FCSA links with masochism/perversion

Psychoanalyst Stoller (1986) discusses female masochism as a phenomenon in which the females deny the expression and release of the sadistic impulse, and instead turns it towards the self as a form of masochism. In the perverse act, childhood sexual trauma is relived, and the trauma is twisted into pleasure and gratification. The perversion becomes an erotic form of hatred, and 'in the perverse act the past is rubbed out' (Stoller, 1986: 6).

His statement supports Glenn's view about mastering trauma through masochism: 'the masochist devised methods of provoking pain, punishment, and torture to prevent narcissistic mortification and other forms of uncontrollable distress' (Glenn, 1984: 359). His term narcissistic mortification refers to Eidelberg's (1968 in Glenn, 1984) idea of an abrupt emotional experience that results in a total loss of control, producing fright and terror for the person. When the superego, ego, and environmental forces indicate that sadism is not appropriate, it may transmute into its opposite, masochism: the eroticisation of a traumatic event. The anxiety it induces and the seduction of the aggressor may serve to alleviate the symptomatology.

The traumatic, painful experiences may be connected to original objects, and the process of needing to establish contact with the original objects will include the desire to reproduce the painful stimulation (Glenn, 1984). Arguably, the masochist's experience of past trauma seems to have a sense of amnesia and dissociation.

The lack of will, agency, and a sense of helplessness can be seen exhibited in both the victim of trauma and the individual with masochistic characteristics. The victim of trauma feels powerless and depends on the tormentor, thus creating the condition of masochism. The masochist submits to the sufferings and abusive relationships as a result of much of the memory and experience connected to the childhood traumatic experience being dissociated and inassimilable. She dissociates rage and aggression and the part of will and agency, which is linked to the dissociated experience, thus detaching the pain that she may have been exposed to during the trauma. The inaccessibility of pain and rage strengthens the incapacity for self-defence and brings understanding to the masochist's passivity (Howell, 1996).

The masochist's sense of self disintegrates, and her perception of being help-less implies that she needs protection. In this process, her dissociated parts of self emerge with her internal self-protector, which has been created by her victim part. The self-protector's task is to protect the individual from further trauma, which may include demanding various behaviours from the individual for the sake of avoiding pain. The self-protector becomes a persecutor who has no attachment. The self-induced torture of masochism is applied by the dissociated part of the self onto the other parts of the self (Howell, 1996).

Howell (1996: 427) proposes that the masochist's psyche may become a tri-partite structure in which all three parties are internalised and dissociated from each other, the 'new tripartite division of the psyche might be postulated: victim self-state, perpetrator self-state, and the self-observer/narrator'. The masochist has dissociated the self-state of the perpetrator mainly by internalising it. To note here briefly, originally, the tripartite system was proposed by Fairbairn (2002).

Often, the only bonding the victim of trauma knew was the traumatic bonding with the aggressor – that violence equals connectedness and organises the masochist's perceptions of intimacy (Miller, 1994), generating the masochist to wish to connect with an object that can tolerate the hostility and separation (Benjamin, 1986). In the process of traumatic bonding, the victim reverses the trauma and becomes the perpe-trator while also remaining the victim. The pain and despair experienced originally by the survivor of the trauma may be aimed at the object thought as containing parts of the self whose existence one has denied (Garland, 2004).

The concept of identification with the aggressor was formulated by Anna Freud ([1936] 1993). She drew her concept from her extensive clinical work with children and their parents. The child attempts, through her identification with the aggressor, to overcome her feelings of helplessness and terror while attaining libidinal grati-fication. She stated that:

> By impersonating the aggressor, assuming his attributes, or imitating his aggres-sion, the child transforms himself from the person threatened into the person who makes the threat.
>
> (Freud, 1993: 113)

The identification with the aggressor's important function, for the ego and the superego, is to restore the psychic equilibrium shaken by trauma (Blum, 1987). The reversal of trauma, as identification with an aggressor, is not merely a desire to relinquish the mental pain into an object-substitute that could bear the turmoil, but it could be the person's only way of communicating her pain through projective identification (Klein, 1946). The projection of pain may function as the person's defensive means of psychic survival. The identification with the aggressor turns towards oneself and can emerge as masochism (Garland, 2004).

Freud (2005) described a narcissistic process in which the ego identifies with a lost object after an overwhelming loss or separation:

> the shadow of the object fell upon the ego, which could now be condemned by a particular agency as an object, as the abandoned object. Thus the loss of object had been transformed into a loss of ego, and the conflict between the ego and the beloved person into a dichotomy between ego-criticism and the ego as modified by identification.
>
> (Freud, 2005: 209)

In other words, the ego becomes the lost object when facing unbearable loss. His theory was further developed by Klein (1946), who identified and formulated the concept of projective identification as a process in which part of the self is experienced as unacceptable, and/or intolerable feelings are triggered by unbearable experiences, and those parts or feelings are split off and projected to the outside world. Garland expands by saying that 'projective identification, as well as being an intrapsychic process..., occurs in a relationship with an external object and affects both the subject and the object' (Garland, 2004: 141). I believe that projective identification is an essential mechanism when explaining FCSA.

Transgenerational abuse may have roots in the history of the offender being victimised or the offender's mother being victimised. A female offender who was sexually abused as a child by a male may act out her shameful feelings of disempowerment, resulting in her identification with her aggressor. She may see her daughter the same way as she regards herself, as devalued, guilty, and unable to escape the experience of sexual abuse. The offender's attempt to imitate her suffered abuse is not a behavioural strategy to replace her own experience of victimisation with control, but an aim to create an intrapsychic event (Turner and Turner, 1994).

Identification with the aggressor is an important dynamic in the life of the victim of CSA. The victim may experience the offender's abusive behaviour as her own behaviour and idealise the perpetrator while denying the abuse. Because of internalising the offender, the child may become aggressive to master the experienced attack (Shengold, 1979).

Rosencrans's (1997) research found that female perpetrators described their mothers as distant, demanding, cold, domineering, weak, and needy. Sexual abuse fulfils some needs of the victimiser, such as gaining power and control, receiving affiliation, and fulfilling sexual needs. This process would be experienced as pleasurable by the perpetrator and projected onto the victim to achieve a perceived well-being. Saradjian (1996) states that the victims will internalise a model to cope with emotional arousal via dominance and victimising others, which may be used as their coping mechanism, especially when experiencing high levels of stress.

A woman's unconscious reservoir of trauma memories can be triggered by any aspect associated with her experienced childhood trauma. Regarding the relationship between sexual trauma, memories, and arousal, Saradjian (1996) suggests that, as a result of conditioning, there is a significant plausibility that the process of memories being triggered can occur with sexual arousal and that this could be linked to a need for revenge for the abuse suffered. Thus, this behaviour is rewarding and can become addictive.

Child as her perverse mother's extension of self

Welldon (2004) has extensively written about how women who have been used as an extension of their mother's bodies repeat that pattern and use their babies as an extension of their bodies. Motz (2008) concurs with Welldon by stating that female perversion lies in the whole body of the woman and the extension of their body. When women engage in the destruction of their bodies, they are essentially seeking the destruction of their cruel mother that they have internally imbibed within themselves. They experience their body as being fused with their mother's body. Furthermore, they abuse their children as they fundamentally see them as a detested extension of themselves. A narcissistic mother who actively enables their child's dependency on the symbiotic bond between them can abet the child to develop masochism. This masochism acts as a mechanism that ensures that the child can satisfy the mother's sadism whilst circumventing the child's fear of losing this bond (Glenn, 1984).

Pines (1993), who has written about a woman's unconscious use of her body through pregnancy, birth, abortion, miscarriage, menopause, and sexuality, argues that a pregnant adolescent mother often projects various aspects and parts of self onto her invisible foetus and regards it as if it were an extension of her body and sense of self. The projections of the young mother are a frequent activity during pregnancy; the birth of her baby may evoke distress in her when she realises her needy baby's separateness from her body. Thus, the baby's birth may stir awareness in the young mother of her unmet needs when she was a baby.

The pregnant woman may experience ambivalent identification with her own mother during her pregnancy, and after giving birth, might still stay in a child position with her own mother. However, if the pregnancy is successful, the resolution of her ambivalent feelings may be successful, and her pregnancy may contribute to building up her sense of femininity and gender (Pines, 1993). Violent mothers' life experiences have been full of deficiency, and many such mothers have an unconscious wish to have a baby to fulfil their sense of inner emptiness, which may be associated with their own childhood experience of the non-existence of a good internal object (Motz, 2008).

Women who have felt undervalued in their gender identity and unconfident concerning their sense of femininity may regard motherhood as a solution to their inner conflicts. Often, those women who have been abused physically, emotionally, or sexually have a low sense of self-worth and cannot gain a sense of independence

(Welldon, 2007a). Welldon (2007a: 63) asserts that for those women, having a baby could be regarded

> as the only way to provide a secure and affectionate bond for themselves…the baby's existence is to gratify mother, and they feel cheated, frustrated, and angry when faced with baby's demands. The mother regresses to her own deprived childhood, identifies with the aggressive mother, and may easily attack the disappointing and depriving child.

Moreover, mothers who have experienced maternal abuse are at increased risk or higher probability of experiencing abusive relationships, which weakens their sense of self-esteem and causes further difficulties in their capability to mother (Motz, 2008).

Although Pines (1993) does not focus on her notion of female perversion, arguably, her idea sheds further light on the development of the woman's vulnerability to using her child's body as an extension of self. She claims that an adolescent mother may use her pregnancies and her babies as a way of fulfilling her psychic vacuum and wishes to gain love from her baby that she never received from her mother or herself. In the process of giving birth, the young mother may find it unbearable to realise that her baby is outside her body and has her own needs to be met. The new mother may start to experience the needy baby as a representative of her own hated parts of the self. She may wish to identify with her mother, and mothering her baby conflicts with her identification with her baby and her search for a narcissistic, infantile state to be mothered again.

Although the momentary regression, especially within the adolescent pregnancy, may be a healthy and necessary process, a young mother's ambivalent early relationship with her mother may cause the regression during the pregnancy to become frightening. This may, in turn, create disturbances in her mothering (Pines, 1993). According to Motz (2008), Pines identified an important distinction, in both practical and psychodynamic terms, between being a mother and experiencing pregnancy. She describes the overriding sense of dismay that women may feel at the birth of their babies. In her words,

> the baby who not only fails to compensate them for their deprivation but also stirs up memories of frustrated needs and infantile rage, can lead to renewed feelings of anger, abandonment and isolation. The unbearable nature of the reactivated pain can lead to violent or perverse assaults on the baby.
>
> (p. 25)

The attacks on the baby have clear sadomasochistic characteristics in which the anger that the mother experiences towards her own mother and herself is directed towards her baby (Motz, 2008).

The survivors of FCSA I interviewed for my MA research (Getu, 2003) give empirical evidence of how the mother attacks her baby with sadomasochistic rage.

They describe their experiences as follows: 'I was always there for her pleasures or wants...my mother was very hard, strict and demanding of me ...', 'constant undermining, shouting, screaming, blaming...Acting out her pain and rage ...we were 'hers'...for her to do as she chose...', 'non-loving',

> female parts were...ridiculed. I was humiliated, and ashamed in front of the people. I had no own life, my needs did not matter most of the time, I didn't think I had any rights: she could do as she pleased with me...volatile, angry, obsessive...

'my mother never tired telling me what an awful evil, bad, "baby slut" I was. She also "threatened me with death"'.

A woman differentiates and becomes an individual within an ongoing relationship, thus making her need for connection function as her primary motivation. Sexual abuse and the lack of attachment may affect the development of empathy, both for others and oneself. It is in that relational context that the woman may commit the abuse by adopting her abuser's characteristics as a way of staying in that relationship. It may also be the female teenage sex offender's attempt to differentiate from her mother's victim identity. A pilot treatment study by Turner and Turner (1994) showed that whenever the daughters tried to set themselves apart from their mothers, the mothers behaved as if they were losing some parts of themselves. They experienced their daughters' attempts to differentiate as negative reflections of their failed ability to separate.

Glasser's general view of the development of perversion

But how does perverse mothering develop into an all-consuming cycle? Although Glasser's (2003) notion of the 'core complex' does not relate directly to women's development of perversion, it is important to examine it, as I believe it will bring further understanding about the development of female perversion.

Glasser (2003) built his understanding of perversion around a notion that he calls the 'core complex'. He starts his investigation of the core complex by exploring aggression, which he claims to be a vital component in perversion. According to Glasser, there is no single definition of aggression, which he claims originally came from everyday language. He presents briefly various outlooks on aggression, such as seeing aggression as a behavioural response or an instinctual drive.

Although Glasser's notion of the core complex is formulated for explaining the development of perversion in both genders, I believe his notion sheds light on the understanding of the development of female perversion, and specifically, the development of FCSA, due to his argument that the mother lies at the core of the development of perversion.

When exploring aggression as an instinctual drive, Glasser refers to Freud's (1905, 1915) method 'in regarding a drive as having a *source,* an *aim* and an *object*…it also has a *stimulus*' (Glasser, 2003: 281). A perverse person feels an intimate longing and a desire to merge in an inclusive state of union with an object that removes all fears and, with great satisfaction, provides complete security against any scarcity and elimination. The long-awaited intimacy entails a completely unfailing containment of any damaging feelings towards the object. Yet, the longed merging stays in a primitive state. For the pervert, merging entails: 'a *permanent* loss of self, a disappearance of his existence as a separate, independent individual into an object, like being drawn into a "black hole"' (Glasser, 2003: 284). The sense of emerging from a temporary state of merging does not exist for the pervert, as merging feels like being swallowed up by the object.

Therefore, the pervert feels the anxiety of becoming annihilated, which is described as the 'annihilatory anxiety' as 'flight from the object, retreating emotionally to a "safe distance" (i.e., essentially, a narcissistic withdrawal)' (Glasser, 2003: 285). This withdrawal from the object leaves the pervert with a sense of desertion, seclusion, and a low sense of worth due to the non-existence of narcissistic provisions, resulting in the aggression being directed towards the self. The felt sense of isolation sets off the pervert to long for a safe and permanent union with the object while triggering the vicious circle of the core complex.

The psychodynamic understanding of the embodied nature of perverse motherhood

Perversion is not seen in this context in psychoanalytic terms as a derogatory word referring to sexual behaviour deprived of genital sexuality. Stoller (1986) gives a useful general definition of perversion linking perversion and erotised aggression. To understand his term perversion, the term aberration introduced by him needs to be explored. He describes aberration as a cluster of procedures that a person uses as their comprehensive sexual act, differing from one's culturally accepted normality of customs.

Variants and perversions comprise the two classifications of an aberration. A variant refers to not being motivated by fantasies of harming others, whilst perversion means 'the erotic form of hatred…' The erotic hatred, when enacted out, is driven by hostility, its main motivation is full deviation, and its goal is to gain full gratification. At the centre of the perverse function is the yearning to hurt others (Stoller, 1986). This is so often seen in the cases of FCSA.

Welldon (2004) challenges the traditional historical thinking by psychoanalytic authors that men were wicked and deviant, whilst women were regarded as neurotic. She claims that female perversion is not genital but lies in the function of the entire female body, including the reproduction of babies. This radical definition of female perversion sheds light on the understanding of FCSA whilst also challenging the traditional psychoanalytic assumption that perversion is related to the phallus.

The meaning of the pervert's behaviour is described in psychoanalytic terms as an incapacity to obtain sexual fulfilment within an intimate relationship. The individual instead is controlled by compulsive behaviour that constitutes an outlet for intolerable sexualised anxiety, and the perverse act must be compulsively repeated in the hope of finding a solution and relief to the psychic conflicts (Lloyd-Owen, 2007). The masochist tries to develop methods of pain that could bring relief to their internal pain caused by trauma (Glenn, 1984) and uses their behaviour to solve the problem between activity and passivity (Benjamin, 1986). The perversion can be seen as resulting from an interaction between hostility and sexual desire, whereby hostility is transmitted through a covert fantasy of revenge that transforms childhood trauma into a mastery of adulthood (Stoller, 1986).

Summary

In this chapter, I wanted to build an understanding of why some women sexually abuse children through an examination of the misogynistic construction of the female. I depict the genesis of the perpetrating mother, as a little girl, who is finding it impossible to discover and treasure her own voice and agency coupled with the absent father, her complying mother, with nobody to turn to. The exploration then widens by inviting the reader to imagine the tumultuous trajectory of the little girl's heartbeat, a little girl who feels sucked in and spat out, enmeshed and deserted, while developing an armour of masochism to manage her anxieties, which emanate from the oscillating dynamic between her desire and apathy. The perpetrating mother's behavioural dynamic develops into a full-blown cycle of perversion and erotic hatred, through which she projects her rage against her own body and her children's. She inflicts sexual abuse through the complex dynamic of enmeshment, whereby the bodies of her children are viewed as being part-objects of herself. It is clear that child sexual abuse serves a function that facilitates both the access and consolidation of power for female perpetrators, as well as channelling their violence, helplessness, and frustrations, ultimately enabling the projection of these conflicting feelings onto those 'mirror images' of themselves: the children. At the end of the chapter, various psychodynamic ideas searching for the answer to the question of why a woman would sexually abuse a child, land firmly on the psychodynamic, embodied foundation through the concept of Welldon.

In the next chapter, the shattering story of the life of Berta, the client I worked with some years ago, will bring to life the theories presented above.

Bibliography

Allen, C. (1991) *Women and Men Who Sexually Abuse Children: A Comparative Analysis*. Brandon: The Safer Society Press.

Arkin, A. (1984) A hypothesis concerning the incest taboo. *Psychoanalysis Quarterly*, 71, 485–500 in Allen, C. (1991) *Women and Men Who Sexually Abuse Children: A Comparative Analysis*. Brandon: The Safer Society Press.

Benjamin, J. (1986) 'The alienation of desire: Women's masochism and ideal love', in Alpert, J. (ed.) *Psychoanalysis and Women: Contemporary Reappraisals*, pp. 113–138. New York: Routledge.

Benjamin, J. (1995) *Like Subjects, Love Objects: Essays of Recognition and Sexual Difference*. London: Yale University Press.

Blum, H. (1987) The role of identification in the resolution of trauma: The Anna Freud memorial lecture. *Psychoanalytic Quarterly*, LVI, pp. 609–627.

Bonaparte, M. (1953) *Female Sexuality*. New York: International Universities Press.

Burgess, A. and Hazelwood, R. (eds.) (1987) *Practical Aspects of Rape Investigation: A Multidisciplinary Approach*. Boca Raton, FL: CRC Press.

Cavanagh Johnson, T. (1989) Female child perpetrators: Children who molest other children. *Child Abuse and Neglect*, 13(4), pp. 571–585.

Chaplan, P. (2005) *The Myth of Women's Masochism*. Lincoln, NE: iUniverse.Inc.

Cleugh, J. (1951) *The Marquis & The Chevalier*. London: Andrew Melrose.

Deutsch, H. (1945) *The Psychology of Women*, vols. 1 & 2. New York: Grune & Stratton.

Fairbairn, W.R.D. ([1952] 2002) *Psychoanalytic Studies of the Personality*. London: Routledge.

Fitzroy, L. (1999) II. Mother/daughter incest: Making sense of the unthinkable. *Feminism and Psychology*, 9(4), pp. 402–405.

Freud, S. (1914) *Remembering, Repeating and Working-through: Further Recommendations on the Technique of the Psycho-Analysis* 11. In The Standard Edition of Complete Psychological Works of Sigmund Freud: Case History of Schreber, Papers on Technique and Other Works. Vol. 12 ([1958] 2001). Translated from the German by James Strachey. London: Vintage Books.

Freud, S. ([1924] 1961) *Standard Edition 19*. Translated from the German by James Strachey. London: Hogarth Press.

Freud, S. ([1933] 1989) *New Introductory Lectures on Psychoanalysis*. Translated from the German by James Strachey. New York: W.W Norton & Company, Inc.

Freud, A. ([1936] 1993) *The Ego and the Mechanisms of Defence*. London: Karnac Books.

Freud, S. ([1955] 2001) *An Infantile Neurosis and Other Works*. The Standard Edition of the Complete Psychological Works of Sigmund Freud. Vol. XVII (1917–1919). Translated from the German by James Strachey. London: Vintage.

Freud, S. ([1917] 2005) *On Murder, Mourning and Melancholia*. Translated from the German by Whiteside, S. London: Penguin Group.

Garland, C. (2004) 'Issues in treatment: A case of rape', in Garland, A. (ed.) *Understanding Trauma: A Psychoanalytical Approach*. London: Karnac Books, pp. 108–122.

Getu, L. (2003) *An Exploration of Female-to-Female Child Sexual Abuse*. MA thesis, City University.

Glasser, M. ([1979] 2003) 'Aggression and sadism in the Perversion', in Rosen, I (ed.) *Sexual Deviation*. 3rd ed. Oxford: Oxford University Press, pp. 279–299.

Glenn, J. (1984) Psychic trauma and masochism. *Journal of American Psychoanalytic Association*, 32(3), pp. 357–386.

Groth, N. and Birnbaum, J. (1979) *Men Who Rape: The Psychology of the Offender*. New York: Plenum Press.

Howell, E. (1996) Dissociation in masochism and psychopathic sadism. *Contemporary Psychoanalysis*, 32(3), pp. 427–452.

Klein, M. (1946) Notes on some schizoid mechanisms. *International Journal of Psycho-Analysis*, 27, pp. 99–110.

Klein, M. ([1957] 1997) *Envy and Gratitude and Other Works, 1946–1963*. London: Vintage.

Koonin, R. (1995) Breaking the last taboo: Child sexual abuse by female perpetrators. *Australian Journal of Social Issues*, 30(2), pp. 195–210.

Lloyd-Owen, D. (2007) 'Perverse females: Their unique psychopathology', in Morgan, D. and Ruszczynsky, S. (eds.) *Lecturers on Violence, Perversion and Delinquency*. The Portman Papers. London: Karnac Books, pp. 101–116.

Mathis, J. (1972) *Clear Thinking about Sexual Deviations.* Chicago: Nelson-Hall Company.

Motz, A. (2008) *The Psychology of Female Violence: Crimes Against the Body.* 2nd ed. London: Routledge.

Miller, D. (1994) *Women Who Hurt Themselves: A Book of Hope and Understanding.* New York: Basic Books.

Mish, F. (ed.) (1983) Webster's Ninth New Collegiate Dictionary. Spring Field: Merriam-Webster. Inc.

Nachmani, G. (1995) Trauma and ignorance. *Contemporary Psychoanalysis,* 31(3), pp. 423–450.

Olivier, C. (1989) *Jocasta's Children: The Imprint of the Mother.* Trans. Craig, G. London: Routledge.

Petrovich, M. and Templar, D. (1984) Heterosexual molestation of children who later became rapists. *Psychological Reports,* 54(3), pp. 811–822. Available at: https://doi.org/10.2466/pr0.1984.54.3.810

Pines, D. (1993) *A Woman's Unconscious Use of Her Body.* New Haven, CT: Yale University Press.

Reik, T. (19410) *Masochism in Modern Man.* Translated by Margaret Beigel and Gertrud Kurt. New York: Farrar & Rinehart, Inc.

Rosencrans, B. (1997) *The Last Secret: Daughters Sexually Abused by Mothers.* Brandon: Safer Society Press.

Saradjian, J. (1996) *Women Who Sexually Abuse Children: From Research to Clinical Practice.* Chichester: John Wiley & Sons.

Scharff, J. and Scharff, D. (1994) *Object Relations Therapy of Physical and Sexual Trauma.* London: Jason Aronson Inc.

Seymour, A. (1998) Aetiology of the sexual abuse of children: An extended feminist perspective. *Women's Studies International Forum,* 21(4), pp. 415–427.

Shengold, L. (1979) Child abuse & deprivation: Soul murder. *Journal of American Psychoanalytic Association,* 27, pp. 533–560.

Stoller, R. (1986) *Perversion: The Erotic Form of Hatred.* London: Karnac Books.

Turner, M. and Turner, T. (1994) *Female Adolescent Sexual Abusers: An Exploratory Study of Mother-Daughter Dynamics with Implications for Treatment.* Brandon: Safer Society Press.

von Sacher-Masoch, L. (1870) *Venus in Furs.* Harmondsworth: Penguin.

Young, V. (1994) 'Women abusers: A feminist view', in Elliott, M. (ed.) *Female Sexual Abuse of Children.* London: The Guilford Press, pp. 100–112.

Warner, S. (2009) *Child Sexual Abuse: Feminist Revolutions in Theory, Research and Practice.* London: Routledge.

Welldon, E. (2002) *Sadomasochism.* Cambridge: Icon Books.

Welldon, E. ([1988] 2004) *Mother, Madonna and Whore: The Idealization and Denigration of Motherhood.* London: Karnac.

Welldon, E. (2007a) 'Why do you want to have a child?', in Alizade, A (ed.) *Motherhood in the Twenty-First Century.* London: Karnac, pp. 59–71.

Welldon, E. (2007b) 'Forensic psychotherapy the practical approach', in Welldon, E. and Van Velsen, F. (eds.) *A Practical Guide to Forensic Psychotherapy.* London: Jessica Kingsley Publishers, pp.13-19.

Chapter 3

Baby Berta

Trapped in the duck decoy

When I met Baby Berta, a 60-year-old woman, for the first time, I was a newly qualified psychotherapist. I was anxious to do a 'good job' with every client by being reflective, empathetic, and open to anything they would bring up during the sessions, whilst maintaining boundaries and focussing on the client and the therapeutic relationship. I learned the basic information about her from the notes of the agency I worked for. Her family history looked like this: her father and her ten-year-older brother died ten years ago, another brother had died one year before Berta was born, and when he was only one year old, and an older sister who moved long ago from the United Kingdom had not had any contact for many years. She had lived with her parents all her life, apart from when she attempted to join a convent in her 20s and after her mother, who was then in her late 90s, went to live in a care home. Her mother died some years before Berta started her therapy with me.

Berta had had counselling during two periods before seeing me. Both had ended due to no availability for further sessions. These experiences had left her feeling distressed. I was allowed to offer her 16 sessions.

Her medical history was complex, and she was medicated with antidepressants and painkillers. The original notes informed that Berta regularly had various appointments with doctors. While her illnesses and medical appointments seemed to trouble Berta, they also appeared to play an important part in her human relationships; to be listened to and not to be abandoned. The notes also informed me that she was seeking therapy because of 'the memories and I can't live in peace'.

The notes also informed me about her sexual abuse history, which will unfold in the first session. Berta had attempted suicide several times when she was in her late 20s and early 30s. Her GP had confirmed that she was not likely to risk of further suicide attempts.

When I met Berta for the first time, she appeared to look almost shockingly babylike. She sat on the chair in front of me, and soon I felt she had become part of the couch she sat on. There was something very impersonal about her, as if she felt like she was just somebody or something. She started the session by talking about her illnesses in detail. The heater was on, the clock moving slowly, and I sensed that telling me her narrative was a comfortable and, in some strange ways, a pleasurable moment for her.

DOI: 10.4324/9781003607007-5

From the age of four, she had been sexually abused by her father. It started during a 'special' visit to her paternal grandparents and lasted until her early 40s. The abuse included sexual intercourse and masturbation. Her father had abused her mainly at home in her mother's absence, but also sometimes when she was at home. He used to tell Berta that she should be thankful that he loved her that way because nobody else would 'love such an ugly child who had glasses and was so fat'. After the age of 13, the sexual abuse had changed mainly to the forms of verbal sexual and sadomasochistic suggestions and accidental brushings on the sexual parts of her body until her hysterectomy in her early 40s, when it changed back to intercourse. The specifically confusing aspect for her was that she had felt at times pleasure when abused. Her father had also been sadistic towards animals in front of her, whilst making sure that her attention was drawn to his sadistic actions.

Her ten-year-older brother had also sexually abused her from the age of 7–12. Yet, it had been highly confusing for her as the abusive brother was also at times a loving brother, the only love she ever received as a child. Sadly, when the abuse stopped, any expressions of love stopped too, and he spoke to her only in derogatory ways, making Berta question whether he had used his kindness as bait to lure her. For Berta, this was incredibly painful, and she would refer to this several times during the sessions. The last time her father abused her was when Berta was in her early 40s, and the abuse happened in her bedroom. Afterwards, she told her mother about the abuse. Her mother, who had been sitting in the rocking chair in the next room where the abuse happened, ignored her, but that is when the abuse finally stopped.

All this heinous abuse, which she described in a disconnected manner as if it were nothing but a matter of fact, had left her feeling confused. I strongly sensed that the disconnection was her way of protecting herself from a further mental breakdown. The initial session left me feeling sad and flooded with empathy; my task was to offer her a space to talk freely and develop a capacity to reflect, help her find her voice, and make her aware that I was traversing her journey with her. However, from the very first session, I had an odd and almost uncomfortable feeling that there was much more under the surface of that babylike demeanour.

Berta came to her second session and was eager to talk. It emerged that Berta had collected 500 specially designed, real-looking baby dolls kept in one of her bedrooms with their clothes neatly arranged and their life stories recorded. Some of the baby dolls slept in her bedroom. Her newest doll was called 'The Crying Baby', about whose cry she spoke with deep emotion and tenderness.

During the rest of the session, Berta quickly switched the topic to her illnesses. Was she hiding behind her illnesses and doctoral visits? Who was Berta? I felt strongly that the doll collection had a deep emotional meaning and symbolism for Berta. Was she, in her imagination, one of the dolls? What aspects did the dolls carry for her? I felt uncomfortable thinking about her sleeping with her baby dolls and changing their nappies and clothes.

She came to her following session on time as always. Her narrative developed. She had tried to separate from her parents by becoming a nun and joining a convent, but 'the good mother superior had turned out to be an uncaring person' and coldly told her to leave the convent. It had been a devastating and rejecting experience as she had wished the convent to provide her a way out from abuse. I wondered whether I was going to be experienced by her as a bad mother (in transference) who would betray and abandon her as her previous mothers/therapists had. However, I kept my thoughts to myself as I felt the therapeutic relationship was not yet established for such in-depth exploration.

Berta talked about her abandoning family and disconnection from communities. I sensed how she had navigated the lonely paths of these losses on her own, without anyone helping her to reflect and make any sense of them. She expressed her concern about what would happen after the sixteenth session. I brought it to the attention of my supervisor, who promised to think about this dilemma. Touched by her despairing isolation, my empathy grew stronger. Where would she have more therapy?

In the fourth session, it surfaced that in her 30s, she had published several children's books, but never felt appreciated by her family as she had never felt regarded as 'good enough'. Instead, her blond and beautiful older sister had been praised for succeeding academically. There had been a rivalry between Berta and her sister, and distinctly, a narrative of one of her books described, by Berta had a fatal rivalry between twins. One of the twins was clever, beautiful, and loved, while the other was not. For me, her books talked about Berta's early-formed inner split. In the supervision, we discussed whether the twins describe a double universal theme in which an ego-ideal searches for an ego-ideal, and one envies what one is not and attempts to kill the double (Kohut, 2009).

When I heard about her published books, I felt strongly that these books existed only in her fantasy to provide her with a space to experience and express her inner conflicts, and maybe to find some resolution by eliminating the desired child. Throughout the sessions, she never brought me the books to show, and the only aspect of them we worked through was the twin rivalry. During several sessions, she reflected on it and found similarities between that murderous rage depicted in the book and what she had felt towards her sister. Her sister had 'escaped' by moving abroad as a young woman.

Berta's mother had been an overprotective mother towards her, and Berta thought it was due to her middle brother's death just one year before her birth. Berta said she had never allowed herself to 'grow up' and separate from her mother. She blamed herself for not separating from her parents. Yes, Berta looked like an overgrown toddler. It was exceedingly challenging to hear how her mother was overprotective whilst letting her father sexually abuse her. My perception widened that her mother had ostensibly used Berta to be sexually abused by her father, and not allowing her to leave home for her own purposes. The session ended with Berta telling how she had wanted to snatch a baby after she had had a hysterectomy and how the dolls had kept her from doing that. She expressed great relief that she had been able to tell me that, and I had a strong feeling not to intervene but to listen. I became more concerned about what else could be hidden behind her mask. Was I the right person to work with her as a newly qualified therapist?

The theme of badness and self-blame became more established in the fifth session. Berta recited her humorous and sad poem called 'The Crying Baby' at the beginning of the session while holding the doll she had brought to the session. The 'not wanted' baby was portrayed as demanding attention, mother's milk, father's money, and making smelly pews. I asked her if she had felt like that about herself, to which she responded quietly that she had not been wanted. She remembered her mother yelling at her father, 'You pushed yourself to me! Pity I couldn't drown her as one drowns the kittens'. (An image came immediately to my mind of how her father had pushed himself into her and penetrated under her skin.) Berta added, 'I was a clinging baby who cried a lot'. Towards the end of the session, I asked whether she had felt clinging to the previous therapists and even me, and then felt abandoned by them, to which she responded that she often felt that with people. She could not express feelings about her mother's betrayal, but she expressed deep hurt from the rejection by the idealised mother figure, the Mother Superior.

Berta blamed herself for her mother being so unhappy – her mother had told Berta that she had to stay in such a horrible marriage because of her. Berta had been made a scapegoat whilst also given an omnipotent, perverted power: her father had 'preferred' to control her sexually over her mother, and her mother had to stay with her father to keep Berta happy. She felt that it was her ugliness and need to be loved that had caused her to be sexually abused and repeatedly stated that all the pain in the family was caused by her badness. It was at a very early age that she had felt she was both an abuser and a victim. The room was filled with a shared silence, and I felt strongly that I was asked to help her carry her burden.

When thinking about Berta's feelings of her badness: producing pew; and demanding milk, the lifeline for the babies, and while being pushed to the corner of a perverse omnipotent position, I found it helpful to think about Fairbairn's (2002) writings of badness and how 'demanding too much' increases one's sense of badness and how it with the sense of impotence adds into complexities and leads to fragmentation and death. The following is a short verbatim towards the end of the fifth session, which shows fractures in Berta's capacity to symbolise:

Berta: I have always imagined things...all the time...
             (*silence*)
Berta: I had an imaginary family. I was with them all the time and they were with me... As a child, I used to play for hours alone. But I was never really alone as my imaginary family loved me. They loved me so much. In that family, I had blond, curly hair and blue eyes. I was a very beautiful child, completely different from who I really was. I had black hair and brown eyes.
I: It seems that you felt comforted by your imaginary family...You got the love from them you didn't get from your real family.
Berta: Yes, I still have them...I still have my imaginary family. I am grown up in that now...I have a father, five brothers, and odd...no mother. My father is not much at home. It's my brothers who love me, especially

the one born before me (*The brother born before the client in the real family had died*). I am the youngest. Some of my dolls are my brother's children.

I: Do you have children in that family?

Berta: I have seven children. My dolls are my children...seven of my dolls. (*She looks ashamed*) I have also adopted children. One is a child whose parents died in a fire after a car crash...they are all like that...two come from a family in which the father killed the mother and then committed suicide...

I felt disturbed and concerned about Berta's strong belief that her imaginary and doll families were 'real'. The sense of her imaginary family was so strong that I had to remind myself to keep referring to it 'as if' and not as an existing reality. It seemed that her capacity to symbolise had been powerfully affected by various traumas. Berta went everywhere with her imaginary family, including her church, where her brothers sat and sang with her in the pews. While she was comforted by having them with her all the time, with the deepening of our therapeutic relationship, she had to leave them outside the therapeutic space, as, according to Berta, they were not happy to come in with her. Did she feel that she had to leave part of her at the doorstep of my therapy room? Or was she feeling freed without their protective shield? I decided not to make direct interventions, at that time, about his imaginative family, as I believed Berta was a very fragile person.

I had seen a glimpse of how Berta had constructed her identity to cope with the devastating effects of being abused for so many years. Hearing about the violence in the histories of her imaginary children: parents getting killed, the father figure committing suicide, and the absence of the mother figure was concerning. Berta's experienced trauma seemed to repeat in various forms within her imaginary family, and through it, Berta wished to retaliate against both of her parents. Yet, she saw her imaginary world as having no pain. When I reflected on the pain, death, violence, and absence of a mother, Berta became quiet and said, 'Yes, maybe you are right...I have always thought that being with my imaginary family is just fun'. Her idealised imaginary world seemed to function as a defence against the painful reality. It appeared to provide a psychic refuge from the outside world: what could not be acted out in the outside world was acted out internally, including loving and being loved, but also violence and despair. Her world had been full of hopelessness, anger, fear, and suffocation. I often felt physically suffocated when listening to her story. The session had a powerful impact as Berta howled for one hour later during the week in the presence of a church elder. Her anguish was starting to find tangible expression through the floods of tears in the presence of an adult man.

Berta hadn't told her previous counsellors about the imaginary family. The trust she had given me felt like a burden with the awareness of having only eleven sessions left. I felt powerless while privileged within the limited time frame. Berta had felt helpless and special when being abused in a 'time without a limit'; more than 40 years of abuse.

I brought up my worry about Berta's mental health state to the supervision group. She had seemingly never been diagnosed as having a mental illness. Despite the daily contact with her imaginary family, she seemed to cope relatively well socially. The discussion of various ways of seeing psychoses in the supervision group reduced some of my anxiety, and the supervision group helped me to think that often a traumatised person cannot differentiate between an 'as if' experience from a real-life experience. The individual experiences a re-enactment of trauma as if it is happening now (Garland, 2004). In the supervision, it was agreed that due to the short-term counselling, we needed to focus on her present life issues, such as her social contacts. However, I felt that ignoring her story about her imaginary family would communicate that her story had been unbearable to me. Hadn't it been unbearable and shameful for her for many years? I felt torn between what Berta wanted to talk about, and what she 'should' talk about.

I tried to shift the sessions to do cognitive work about her self-esteem and focus on any social events, but she insisted on talking about the various traumas. I felt an increasing sense of being between two choices: to facilitate a brief therapy or to be led by my client. It felt like I was in an impossible place. I reflected on how I must have introjected a sense of Berta's dilemmas of having impossible choices she had experienced all her life, yet my impasses had no likeness to hers.

But the imaginary family stayed in the centre and filled the room; it felt as if it was dominating her mind, and each time she talked about it, her eyes closed, and her breath became heavy. Her narratives and her absence from the therapy room made me feel concerned about her mental stability and strong capacity to dissociate, and I saw it was necessary to bring her back to the present environment. Berta's body seemed to speak by closing her eyes and having the illnesses speak what her words couldn't speak.

During the sessions, Berta displayed a complete lack of grief and emotions when talking about her painful experiences. It seemed that she had experienced a breakdown in her grieving process. When asked whether she felt angry towards her family, she responded, 'It was right I got punished'. At this moment, I could have encouraged exploration about punishment, but my countertransference informed me that such a question could feel like a punishment, too. I was also concerned about opening issues that could be difficult to close within the time limit. Later in the therapy, we talked several times about her feelings of guilt.

By this time, I had many thoughts and questions: the seductiveness and controlling power of her stories, what was real/fantasy, her stagnated grief, and the splits of her identity. Were the dolls her internal objects, and did some of them need to die to symbolise the losses in her life? What about the lack of a mother and Berta seeing herself as the idealised mother to her baby dolls? Was I going to be the idealised mother or the bad/absent mother?

I continued having a conflict between keeping Berta focussed on present 'real life' issues while not hindering her from sharing about her imaginary family. Had she not always experienced that conflict: What was real and what was not real? Had she not wondered whether her mother, father, and brother loved or didn't love her? So, Berta talked more about her relationships with her mother and father. She had always felt suffocated in her mother's presence, not appreciated, not 'good enough', and not protected while over-protected. Her mother had always put her needs before Berta's, making it impossible for Berta to separate from her. Berta had never learned to trust other people's and her own intentions.

As the sessions progressed, Berta increased her eye contact. Her manner of talking also became livelier and more expressive, especially when talking about the abuse. I didn't experience her anymore as being part of the furniture. In the ninth session, her narratives about the splits within her identity became clear. There seemed to be an abusive triangle of positions: an abusive, sadistic father (brother), an absent/abusive mother, and the victim child/abusive adult self, re-enacted in Berta's present identity. It seemed that at times she had no sense of any good objects within her being.

There had been periods in her life when she had wanted to hurt babies. Her desire had been so great that she had planned to keep a book about hurting styles and dates. Yet, she said she had never acted upon her desires as the dolls had stopped her from acting out. She had never wanted to hurt her dolls and her imaginary babies. When I asked how she felt about telling me that she wanted to hurt babies, she responded, 'I feel nothing, absolutely nothing. Of course, I am happy I never hurt anyone'. I was greatly relieved knowing she had no contact with any minors and could not move around without help.

In the last session before becoming my private client (agreed by the agency on session eight), her story changed as she told me she had hurt babies by pinching them and shaking their prams, which she, at the time, had shared with the pregnant GP who had shown disgust. I was left with a sense of being betrayed, disgusted, and trapped for the next 'forty years' in the hands of Bertha and her sadistic abuse/victim behaviour.

She started revealing her abusive behaviours towards children. She had hated her friend's baby, whom she had profoundly envied for being wanted. Berta said,

> Once, I think I pushed her, and she started to cry. I suddenly felt love for her and wanted to comfort her...Other times, I hated her so much. The only thing that kept me away from hurting her more was that I knew I had all the power to do it unconstrained. I was in control. Her parents trusted me fully. I didn't want to lose my power by hurting her...But I really didn't want to hurt babies. It was more about that they were loved that I hated.

It was her omnipotent sense of control that had stopped her from hurting babies more severely. Through that single event of pushing her friend's baby, she lost her omnipotent power and touched humanity through the baby's tears. It seemed that in that moment, Berta could be in touch with the helpless, distressed, and crying child within herself. The original trauma had been re-enacted. Berta had immersed herself in all three positions: the victim, the abusive father, and the absent/abusive mother who didn't protect her.

I made an intervention: the abusive part of her wanted to hurt the vulnerable part of herself, and when hearing the baby crying, she was also comforting herself while comforting the crying baby. She looked down, looked sad, and said that maybe that was the case. But I also sensed that she had felt disappointed that her story had not caused in me great excitement and disgust. I, on the other hand, felt empowered by my interpretation. Hadn't I felt powerless for several sessions? The issue of power had entered the therapeutic relationship in tangible ways.

Berta repeatedly told a story of how a young male nurse in the hospital (where she had been treated) gave her sex education and brought her a sex education book that had drawings of sex acts. She claimed that she still did not know what happened during sex and wanted me to describe the sex acts during the session. Each time this happened, I felt strong nausea and stopped her from embracing her abusive power over me and herself. My countertransference in those moments was disgust and suffocation, which she must have felt when being sexually abused.

The ending

I was convinced she wanted to tell me more than she had been able to, and it was clear to me what she wanted to talk about. But as it happened, she was diagnosed with a terminal illness and became seriously ill after three months of seeing me privately and was taken into a care home. I thought that this was the end of seeing her, but one day, her GP phoned me and asked me to contact her as she desperately needed more sessions. So, I changed the frame of the sessions a second time, and I started seeing her in her care home. We agreed to have only six sessions, and in the third and fourth sessions, she was silent. I reminded her that we had only two sessions left. In the fifth session, Berta was different. It was as if she had been waiting for me and was ready to talk. Just a few minutes before the end of the session, she stated that she had to tell me something she had never told anyone: she had sexually abused three small sisters, one by one, for some time when she was their nanny. She then asked if I saw her differently now. And I answered 'no' as her perpetrated abuse had been revealed to me for some time. During the last session, Berta did not speak. That was the last time I saw her.

Postscript

As Berta's identity and life were divided, so was my relationship with her. While I felt suffocated during the sessions, I equally felt greatly disgusted outside the sessions, specifically when she got a bladder infection, and the stinking and pervasive old urine smell seemed to enter my body long before she entered the room. Yet, the disgust was not about her as a person; it was what she carried within herself about herself and her life. Her pain had gone under my skin.

With sadness, I think about the four little victims: baby Berta and the adult Berta's toddler victims. I grieve over Berta's life and what her life could have been. She had managed to memorialise the lost Baby Berta in her physical statue to tell not only the untold story of her infancy but also her decayed adulthood. Her childhood grief and robbed life stayed imprinted on her face. One may wonder how I, as a survivor, managed to care for her. But I believe it is because of that, I could care for her without fear and hesitation. I think that by the time I knew what she had done, I had already been touched by her core vulnerability, her grief, and the total deprivation of what could have become of her life.

Her life can be depicted as an entrapment from being born into a duck decoy: the little duckling gravitates towards her home waters, involuntarily trapped by the seductive familiarity of its landscape. There was no one to rescue her; neither the Mother Superior nor her GP heard her cry. The therapy room became an extension of an intra-psychic duck decoy, where Bertha, not on her own but together with me as her therapist, re-examined the horrors, grieved her losses, and explored ways to escape her internal torture. Her final flight route was offered to her in the form of impending death. I can see it now plainly, how the therapy led to that significant point of me being a priest to whom she needed to confess before dying.

Bibliography

Fairbairn, W.R.D. ([1952] 2002) *Psychoanalytic Studies of the Personality.* London: Routledge.

Garland, A. (ed.) (2004) *Understanding Trauma: A Psychoanalytical Approach.* London: Karnac Books.

Kohut, H. ([1971] 2009) *The Analysis of the Self: A Systemic Approach to the Psychoanalytic Treatment of Narcissistic Personality Disorder.* Chicago, IL and London: The University of Chicago Press.

PART II

Clinical implications

Section 1

Between Scylla and Charybdis

Chapter 4

Ruth struggles with the Five-Headed Monster

The relational splits

Introduction

By applying a lens of dissonant imagery present in the Voyage of Odysseus, the granular complexity of the relational splits that Ruth faces becomes clearer. I will refer to the Five-Headed Monster as both a visual representation and a guide to deconstruct and establish the relational variables Ruth is navigating and experiencing. Who is this Five-Headed Monster? Alive and so fluidly moving. The monster kicks and splits itself into invisible yet tangible formations among the staff members in the ward where Ruth works. It moves powerfully within Ruth, and its pervasive impact is felt within the therapeutic relationship between Ruth and her client as if its power has eclipsed the essence of her client's being. These splits are further produced by the overriding social landscape that surrounds her, particularly within her relationship to society. Society, at large, is blinded by the normalising lullabies that conceal FCSA. In Ruth's experience, the relational splits created by FCSA seem to be felt within every relational dynamic that Ruth encounters through her work with her client Kathy.

Splitting is:

> to divide (persons) into different groups, factions, parties, etc., as by discord.
> (American Psychological Association, 2017)

Ruth's experience of relationships with her colleagues; the conflicts within herself about her client; and her therapeutic relationship with Kathy were at times full of tensions and conflicts, whilst also being saturated with truthful empathy. The contradictions within her client, as experienced by Ruth, and the splits in understandings on a societal level regarding FCSA were tangible. The word split encompasses Ruth's myriad experiences of relationship/s on the ward. This included her own divided experience of the professional psychologist Ruth versus the woman Ruth, who feels compelled to conceal her womanhood, versus the manifestation of how her subjective vantage point behaves. In the case of Kathy, her perception regards her client's characteristics as being divided into two or multiple parts.

DOI: 10.4324/9781003607007-8

Splits between the team members

A picture emerges of a team that was extremely polarised in their views about the client: to some, she was a victim and to others, she was an evil manipulator. Ruth herself did not want to fall into this trap of polarising the client, wanting to be able to hold both aspects of her in mind. Understanding the splits between the team working with FCSA is imperative, as it enables us to understand the theoretical implications that it holds. It asserts the fundamental necessity of understanding how boundaries are broken during abuse and how that same intrusive dynamic permeates the therapist's work. To avoid the danger of re-enactment, it is essential to have firm boundaries when working with mother/female child sexual abuse (M/FCSA).

Ruth portrays a picture of the staff members as having multiple and extreme opinions of Kathy, who, at times, was hated by the rest of the team. There was no peace in the ward concerning Kathy. There was struggle and confusion, a sense of a battle, and Ruth was part of that battle. In fact, she experienced Kathy as a difficult person to work with. Ruth's voice echoes here as open and not pretentious at all about the experienced struggles with Kathy '…she was a very difficult person to work with in the sense that she was very much vilified by the rest of the team, I think people really struggled to work with her because of what she had done,…' Working with Kathy essentially meant facing various types of demons, including those belonging to Ruth.

The rest of the team was in turmoil and vilified Kathy. A person who is vilified is degraded and spoken badly about. The word *vilified* evokes many thoughts: why was the team so vicious about her? Did Kathy deserve such treatment? Yet, the staff treated her with contempt for what she had done and perceived her through her perpetrated sexual abuse of children, thus affecting their capacity to work with her. There is a sense that some of the staff abandoned their duty of professionalism/care and became bullies towards Kathy, who was supposed to be cared for by them. Visceral, primitive, and conflicting feelings seemed to have been evoked in the staff team.

It became evident that the team members were divided along their respective polarising moral and emotional positions regarding Kathy. The predominant question contributing to this polarity was whether Kathy was a victim or an evil manipulator. As Ruth says, 'People were very extreme about her, so on one extreme was she this evil manipulative person who abuses all the time and can't be trusted with anything…then there were a lot of people who felt sorry for her…'

Expanding on how these two extreme polarities presented within the team, from one perspective, she was regarded as a thoroughly evil manipulator, a monster, who abused others all the time; from another, she was considered a victim, someone one felt sorry for. When relating to Kathy, the staff members were cast to the furthest edge of their beings, tested in every sense of the word. This determining dynamic of simultaneously conflicting views cumulatively resulted in the staff resorting to extreme defences. Within the context of this overarching dynamic, the cycle of abuse is repeated: the abuser versus her victims; the evil and the one the evil has tarnished. Importantly, in the context of the vertical professional relationship between the staff and Kathy, the staff perceived and experienced these polarities in the same person, Kathy.

The team's views were further divided concerning fear of her re-offending as Ruth says, 'people didn't want to think of her being at risk of reoffending in the future, there was real kind of polarized views towards her...They were all quite extreme'.

Concerning Kathy being regarded as a victim, some of the staff positioned themselves on the extreme end, to the extent of denying any likelihood of her further offending. Merely thinking about it was seemingly too disturbing. The staff's polarised views would have impacted their work with Kathy. Refusing to recognise and evaluate the possibility of the perpetrator re-offending, denies in a way the initial offending too: it never happened and will never happen.

This extreme position, incapable of accommodating the possibility of re-offence, operated in stark contrast with the opposing view of her as essentially evil. This perceived evil that was experienced by some of the team was specifically located within the inter-relational dynamic with Kathy. Kathy drew pictures to be given to the staff members' children: maybe wishing her images, emotions, and physical presence to be carried out from the ward to the staff members' homes. The pictures seemed to have been regarded as incendiary, embodying the perceived evilness of Kathy. The idea of Kathy wanting to give a part of herself to the staff members' children seems to have caused enormous and explosive existential anxiety, which was so overwhelming that they had to wipe not just Kathy's drawings, but Kathy herself from their minds, as if she did not exist. Ruth describes it as '...for people who have had children in the ward they've often said couldn't bear the thought of her or the fact that she draws pictures for their children, and it was really bad'.

The splitting in the ward was tangible as Ruth explains it,

Umm so I was very much aware..., and thinking, you know, almost forcing myself in the beginning,..., I've got to be the one as the psychologist, you know, to be able to hold all that really...I was much more conscious of my own feelings working with her, not to fall into the trap that other people had done, that she was this evil person.

A split is delineated between therapists who fall into the trap of essentialising the client as evil, versus therapists who are capable of holding the spectrum of all that the client is, without resorting to blanket categorisation of the client as evil. Ruth's usage of the word *trap* necessitates a degree of deconstruction. A reasonable starting point would be to regard and accept a trap as being orchestrated by someone. Who has designed this trap? Society at large; the client; the staff? I believe that the important question is how each of us is part of that trap-making. Do we fall into the rigid ways of thinking and labelling women who have been perpetrators of FCSA? Do we turn a blind eye to the fact that FCSA does happen? Was it too much for the staff to remember that Kathy was both the perpetrator and the victim of the abuse?

Whilst Ruth was aware that some people regarded Kathy as evil, she felt professional pressure as a psychologist not to see her that way. As a professional, she was conscious that falling into the trap of labelling her client was a possibility, yet it remained a clear-cut 'must' not to fall into it.

Ruth wanted to be dissimilar to her team members whilst forcing herself to do what she did not want to do – to see her as all bad or evil. This pressure created something akin to violence towards herself. She felt an internal pressure to take a position of holding: must do that; must do the right thing; 'do or die'.

Splits within herself

However, the splits were not just between Ruth and other staff members; they were also within Ruth herself, as Ruth had to force herself at times to work with the client. The split within Ruth is illustrated: she was a therapist versus a woman who hides her womanhood. Ruth protected her womanhood = that is, her status as a female who may have children and did not want her client to see any of it (her private life) by keeping it intact and away from evil. Whilst Ruth could understand her client intellectually, she could not understand her emotionally.

Ruth felt a huge pressure from outsiders to be the one who would fix Kathy, and experienced being placed on a pedestal as a saviour: an embodied symbolic fixer, a psychological magician. She says,

> There was probably pressure from outside to sort of fix her in a way, and I became the symbol of fixing her,…it's the psychology that's going to get you out if you engage…so it put a ridiculous amount of pressure on me to deliver something.

Was the pressure put on her by Ruth herself? And did calling the pressure 'ridiculous' reduce some of her anxiety to be the perfect psychologist? In any case, there is a sense that Ruth being in that idealised position served to reduce the group's anxieties. The assumptions of society, including professionals, can be extreme: the FCSA perpetrator is evil, but the psychologist can fix such a person and turn her away from her evilness. Yet, Ruth does not pretend to be born with such rather unnatural gifts. There is a desperate wish to transform a terrifying person, a woman who sexually abuses children. What about Ruth, the private person? Is she above all that turmoil? There seems to be a clear need for Ruth to keep specific parts of herself intact and protected,

> …and it just everything about it just felt so…it made me personally not want to reveal anything about me as a woman and even though I don't have children, I didn't want her to think or know that I might have.

Hesitatingly, Ruth describes guarding her womanhood and not wanting to reveal anything about it, to hide it behind a veil. She does not say that she did not reveal anything of herself; nevertheless, she divided herself consciously into Ruth, the female therapist, and Ruth, the woman with womanhood, which included the qualities of being a woman, or particularly, with reproductive capacities. Kathy, a woman who sexually assaulted young female children, and Ruth was once a young female child. This attempt at protection in the form of 'concealed' womanhood was essential for Ruth.

Ruth was unequivocal in her stance and did not even want her to imagine her having any children. The idea of Kathy envisaging Ruth having children, although non-existent, seemed to instil in Ruth a feeling of being invaded and contaminated by her client's perversity. Ruth was extremely firm about not connecting with her client in terms of being 'revealed' as a woman, 'that's why I didn't want her in my life'. Her client had to be kept outside, and she did not want the power of perverse imagination to invade her life. As Ruth describes,

> For some reason it didn't affect me, I think there was something about the work and something about the unit I was under at the time, that I just probably I think I just shut it off…I probably made more of an effort not to really think about It and I think that's probably because I don't want to think about it being in my life outside, that the only way I can deal with it is by thinking that's all in there, all that perversion, evilness, nastiness is all kept in hospital and my life doesn't have any of it. And I think that's probably the way I've probably dealt with a lot of the things in my work, that I've kept it locked up in a secure unit on a conscious level… And also, because she lives a long way away, and I don't live in the same town, so I feel I've got that distance as well.

Ruth does not finish her sentence when talking about leaving her client locked inside a secure unit. Splitting her private life from her professional one is a conscious process: a part of her does not want to think about the possibility of abuse being in her life; all the nastiness must be kept in the hospital, in the locked place of care and healing, and Ruth's life has none of that. Having physical distance creates a perception of psychological distance. Although Ruth says that her private life has not been affected by her work, it seems evident, based on the previous extract, that her life has been powerfully affected by her need to split her private life into a place of safety in such totality.

> I think there's a part of me that doesn't want to think about it as well, that it's all in there, you know, it's not all out, otherwise, maybe I'm frightened as well in thinking that, it could be everywhere. Maybe that's just too horrible to think about.

If she were to allow her thoughts about her client to penetrate her private life, Ruth fears that all that horrible 'evilness' could be everywhere, not just consigned to her professional life. She would have no means to contain it, so it is easier to imagine that there is no abuse outside the hospital unit. Her wish to deny that FCSA happens in society, regardless of 'the evilness' being locked inside the secure unit or not, points towards a need for diffusing the dissonance, ultimately enabling an adaptive process of being able to function within and outside the remit of working with Kathy. Working with FCSA perpetrators impacts those who are part of it by penetrating and changing the workers' private lives and beliefs. The therapist needed to make a conscious choice to leave her work outside her private life. The split is not taking place nor functioning in a vacuum, exempt from awareness and decision-making processes. Ruth breaks down how she managed this process of what felt like essential splitting.

> So on an intellectual level, you can understand what had happened. But to connect with her as a person was quite difficult…that's why, and I think I probably ended up being emotionally quite detached in the sense…not cold or maybe I was quite cold, but I just thought I couldn't let you in. Whereas that might be unconscious with other people, I was very much aware of that.

Ruth consciously separates her intellectual and emotional systems of processing. She can carry this out through understanding and engaging with her client intellectually, whilst concurrently emotionally distancing herself from her. The purpose of the distancing mechanism seems to be twofold: helping to protect herself by not letting her client into her life and enabling Ruth to continue to understand her client rationally and challenge her. Ruth is aware that she might have appeared emotionally quite cold whilst doing that. I think this is a clear reference to the fear of sexual abuse being re-enacted, 'I can't let you in', i.e., 'I cannot be the child whose mind and body you might penetrate'. The next sub-theme explores how the splitting happened within the therapeutic relationship.

Splits within the therapeutic relationship

Ruth's difficulties connecting with her client, who appeared childlike and seemed almost incapable of abusing, are apparent. She could almost lull herself into believing that there was no need to explore the abusive part of the client, whilst also jumping at times from seeing her client as very vulnerable to suddenly viewing her as cruel. In Ruth's words,

> It was very strange, and I think because she tried to deny talking about the abuse for a long time, she categorically refused to talk about it. You could get lulled into thinking that you didn't have to go there.

The beginning was strange due to Kathy's refusal to talk about the abuse, so even Ruth could get lulled into thinking that they did not need to talk about it. Ruth felt she was being seduced into a space of not verbalising the abuse and becoming a childlike person herself. The word 'lull' means 'to cause to sleep or rest: SOOTHE'; 'to cause to relax vigilance'; to *lull* people 'into a false sense of security' (Merriam-Webster.com Dictionary, 2025: no page). The children are lulled to sleep, and they can be lulled into being sexually abused. That happened to Kathy, and she then did the same to her victims. In this context, being lulled implies perverse nurturing. Ruth describes how,

> She was a very difficult person to connect with... (long pause)...And she was almost very childlike and sort of unsophisticated herself, and so it was quite hard for me to think of what she'd done, cause, I didn't see that side. She presented herself as quite hopeless and very childlike...and to think that she'd actually done something like that. You could almost trick yourself into believing that that had not happened.

The application of the word *unsophisticated* connotes a person who is straightforward, not capable of plotting evil things. Connecting with that contradiction of innocent childlikeness and perversion constituted a challenge for Ruth. Was Ruth supposed to connect with the childlike person, the sexual perpetrator, or with both? Ruth could, in effect, trick herself into believing the abuse never happened because of the impression of innocence presented by Kathy. There is a parallel here with the victims who often feel and/or are told by the perpetrator that the abuse never happened, and/or it was not abuse. Kathy may also have been an actual victim, yet being childlike does not mean she was without aggression, sexuality, or malevolent intent. Ruth is conflicted by the entrenched contradictions, 'It felt very frustrating because I felt in some ways, she would just go on this denial path, and I'd become more and more entrenched, and I'd then become almost like the abuser in a way...'

Kathy kept on denying her perpetrated abuse, and Ruth became determined that they needed to talk about it. It seems that they were firmly ingrained in their fixed positions on opposite ends of the pole.

> I wonder how much you've given me (meaning Kathy) what I wanted to hear. And now I think sometimes, I did get trapped in that unhealthy dynamic of being quite...I don't want to use the word bullying that's a bit strong but pushing more than I would do with other people, probably just to get some sort of acknowledgment of what she had done, to see that she was aware, maybe that went too far, maybe sometimes I asked her that one question just to try and get some connection to what she'd actually done.

Ruth explored the notion of being trapped in an unhealthy dynamic several times, thus showing that it became an important issue. The 'trap' within this extract comes from Ruth feeling as if she had become an abuser by pushing her client to acknowledge her perpetrated abuse. Ruth wonders whether she asked that question too often, and if it became like an unwanted penetration towards her client. This could be seen as a form of projective identification with Kathy's invasive, intrusive, abusive side. 'That's why I left her at the door because I just thought I'm never giving you anything, not that I disclosed anything anyway but I just thought you're not going to get into my life'.

Ruth reflects on the difficult and complex relationship with her client with such honesty. And I wonder whether her honesty helped her to work through her struggles. I sense sadness when Ruth says that she left her client at the door. Yet, Ruth did not leave her outside the door: outside the home of a therapeutic relationship: she says, 'we could only meet each other kind of halfway…' They met at the doorstep if using an analogue of a house, but out of the door of her own home and her own experiences of motherhood and personal life. I find this heartbreaking and very moving: those two women, the therapist who hides her womanhood and even wants to protect her non-existent children from her client's imagination, meet the other woman, the one who has sexually manipulated and abused small children, at the doorstep, not inside and not outside, but halfway. That is 'good-enough' therapy for Ruth within a danger zone.

Splits within her client

The client presented herself as having extreme polarities. She was childlike while disclosing her abuse in the ward to get more attention or revealing her unconscious need for punishment by being bullied by others, many of whom had been victims of sexual abuse themselves. The client denied the abuse she had perpetrated and presented herself as powerless, whilst she had all the power over her victims. This oscillating behaviour depicts a picture of how Kathy exercised two sides of her personality: a powerful sex abuser and a vulnerable and hurt child.

> She presented herself as quite pathetic, wanted help all the time, she was very needy and very desperate for help and any sort of attention and then there was another side that could be quite cruel, very violent, and aggressive…she was always self-harming, always falling, trying to get people to help her. She said that she didn't know how to wash herself, and she wanted physical care from the staff to wash her. So, she was very perverse in lots of ways; she would disclose her offence to people in the ward so that she could be attacked and bullied, and then she would be on special observation, so she'd get special care.

Ruth paints a picture of a drama of perversion and vulnerability. The staff/patients viewed Kathy as desperately and constantly needy; presenting herself as a child who was falling and incapable of washing herself. The other side of her is depicted as an aggressive, violent, and perverse person who would disclose her offences to other patients and then be bullied and punished by those she attacked. One could also say 'the others' experienced Kathy as presenting herself as a victim, then as a perpetrator, and again as a victim who needed help. The trauma cycle would keep reproducing itself. It was within this context that Ruth had to work with her complex client.

The staff had to work with her client's extreme vulnerability whilst also knowing that at any time they could be at the receiving end of being violated and attacked by her, by the same person they tried to care for. There was also awareness that Kathy could psychologically attack the other patients through disclosures of sexual abuse or sexually abusive thoughts. Who was the staff to protect and rescue? Themselves, and/or Kathy from herself or those she had attacked?

Splits within the society

The splits of society are evident: the denial of FCSA's existence, whilst regarding female sexual abusers as monsters and different from male abusers. Ruth argues that society's assumptions of FCSA offenders enable the abuse to go on,

> Uh and it made me think well here's someone who has come up that we know about, to deny it or as I said I try not to think about it outside, it's doing an in- justice and it's also not acknowledging that women are just as capable of com- mitting violence and sexual offences as men are and that there are so many...

The socio-cultural systemic conditioning of the denial of women's capability to sexually inflict harm does indelible injustice to women as a whole, and I believe, also to men. The belief that women are incapable of such abuse creates an image that they are somehow a more untainted gender than men. It depicts men as the sole carriers of such a horrible shadow side. This universal denial has far-reaching repercussions on the societal level, which Ruth elucidates,

> you know, for the victim, but also the perpetrators as well, that here are people committing offences. And the services aren't developed for people that do these sorts of things, and I think it is because it's so easy for women to slip under the radar, women have so much more access to children, and so much could happen that could be dismissed. How do you know if a cuddle is a cuddle...it's so much more difficult when it's a woman than when it's a man. It made me think, they got to be seen on the same level and understanding as opposed to denigrating and people saying this person is evil, a monster, and different from everyone else. It stops you from thinking that this really happens if you think this case is just a one-off.

Ruth asks, 'How do you know if a cuddle is a cuddle...?' The question she asks reverberates strongly throughout the landscape of FCSA. How does the victim tell others that the cuddle was not a cuddle devoid of sexual wishes; how does society, and even any therapist, believe her? Women have easy access to children, and sex- ual abuse could be dismissed because women are often seen as the 'rightful' carers of children, which makes it harder to recognise sexual abuse as being perpetrated by women. However, if both genders are not seen as equally capable of commit- ting FCSA, the necessary facilities will not be developed to treat those women who sexually offend. Consequently, there remains a great need to acknowledge that women have aggressive and sexual impulses that can take the form of sexual feelings and actions related to children.

The damaging denial of FCSA results in a failure to establish the necessary pathways needed to identify and address FCSA on multiple fronts, from policy intervention to cultural norms. On the one hand, services at best are inadequate or not developed at all to help either victims or perpetrators. On the other hand, labelling women as *evil* prevents a serious engagement with FCSA. This culminates in reproducing further denial about the seriousness of female sexual abuse, as well as relegating and reinforcing FCSA as an outlier, a behavioural phenomenon that separates it from the normative definition and understanding of sexual abuse.

Discussion on the perspectives of splitting

Ruth experiences deep and conflicting tensions between the team members, as well as within both herself and her client, Kathy, the therapeutic relationship, and finally, within society. The child sexual trauma and working with female offenders divide the staff working on the secure unit into various sub-groups, and Ruth also experiences splitting about her work with Kathy. It is important to note that in descriptive terms, instead of using the word 'splitting', the word 'divided' could be used interchangeably.

Ruth talks about splitting between the team members several times. She describes the team as being divided into polar opposites concerning how they view Kathy and how it impacts their work. When exploring the literature, I didn't find any material specifically relating to splitting among staff working within a FCSA perpetrator secure unit. As a result, I have concentrated on examining two areas that I view as key: how staff members respond to the manifestation of anxieties systemically within caring institutions, as well as how working with FCSA female offenders, including those who have murdered their babies, has impacted the staff.

There is a rich body of literature on splitting in psychoanalysis. Nevertheless, it is important to note that it was Klein who wrote most comprehensively about splitting. According to her, splitting, for an infant, is vital to its psychic function and development, but if used profoundly and rigidly, it becomes unhelpful (Klein, 1997). Menzies (1988), in her profound study, found that institutions sanctified defences to keep the nursing staff from feeling the emotional pain of their work. Splitting became part of the working culture. Her findings indicated that firstly, defences were secured, and anxiety did not enter awareness, and secondly, the relationships between patients and staff were damaged, and the nurses' ability to do their work was impacted.

Hinshelwood and Skogstad (2005) argue that staff bring into their workplace their anxieties, and they can be drawn to work within a specific area because their private defences conform with the organisation's characteristics of dealing with its societal defences. Further understanding is gained by Motz's (2008) investigation into staff working within women-only services. She maintains that the staff might have been motivated to work with such services with the overriding desire and goal to restore and save them. This desire to restore stems from the staff maintaining an inherent idealisation of these women – essentially seeing them as vulnerable victims of men. Motz explains how this idealisation is shattered when aggression inevitably surfaces in these women, resulting in a response of disappointment and even retaliation from the staff.

How do staff members process their own anxieties, those of other staff members, and/or patients? Hinshelwood and Skogstad (2005), referring to Menzies' findings, elaborate further on how the externalisation of anxieties, especially about responsibility, is very common. Internal conflict becomes an external one, thus reducing anxiety at the individual level. However, such projections lead to opposing conflicts between distinct parties, preventing the potential for relevant resolutions (Hinshelwood and Skogstad, 2005: 6). Ruth felt extremely responsible, as a psychologist, to hold everything together, thus relieving the other staff members from the anxiety of carrying any responsibilities to 'fix' the client.

Fully committed to being a good and responsible professional, Ruth was unswerving and did not fall into the trap of developing polarised views of Kathy. She did not split off all her anxieties and locate them in her client. At the same time, there is a sense that the other staff members used '*projective identification...* where parts of the self...are not taken in, but instead split off and projected into an object outside of self' (Lemma and Levy, 2004: 19).

On the ward where Ruth worked, the staff's existential anxiety is visible. They plunged into the terror of imagining the possibility of their children being contaminated by Kathy. They dealt with this terror by resorting to wiping her out of their minds, to the extent of denying her existence. Stolorow provides a powerful existential viewpoint on how trauma shatters everyday 'peaceful existence' and our capacity for life.

> ...emotional trauma produces an affective state...it accomplishes this by plunging the traumatized person into a form of authentic being-toward-death. Trauma shatters the absolutisms of everyday life that evade and cover up the finitude, contingency, and embeddedness of our existence and the indefiniteness of its certain extinction.
>
> (Stolorow, 2008: 8)

The longing for intimacy and wanting to stay isolated can be seen as a reflected split among both the patients and staff members. Motz's (2008) illustration of a conflict on the ward between the workers and female patients, diagnosed with a severe personality disorder, is highly relevant. She gives a sensitive description of the diametrical internal conflict that the female patients are battling with. On the one hand, they are constantly desiring intimacy, to be known, and on the other, they are defiantly defending themselves against it, choosing to stay isolated. She asks,

How are staff members to work with this paradox? And how to begin to address the reflected split in this staff group as they struggle with the desires to help, contain and comfort, conflicting with the equally strong urges, at times, to abandon, disappoint and retaliate against these women?

(Motz, 2008: 330)

Ruth went through the experience of being put on a pedestal as the all-fixing psychologist. She attempted to reduce some of that anxiety by calling the pressure 'ridiculous'. The word 'probably', relating to the pressure coming from outside, alludes to the pressure not only emanating from the staff but from Ruth herself.

In the face of this complex and desperate working situation, there is an overwhelming sense that the galvanising of hope is essential. Lemma rightly states that 'the transference relationship is one vehicle for hope' (Lemma, 2004: 124). Klein pointed out that the 'idealization [of the object] derives from an innate feeling that an extremely good breast exists...' (Klein, 1997: 193). Ruth, the professional psychologist, became a good object for herself and others. She became the 'all-containing' professional while hiding away her womanhood from her client. Her splitting was a conscious act to protect herself while protecting others.

As specified by Motz, therapeutic work between a pregnant therapist and a female child killer creates an extremely complex therapeutic relationship. She writes about women who have killed their babies:

...as well as the possibility of an enhanced intimacy and depth in the therapy, as issues that may have been left unexplored like the therapist's sexuality are thrust into the consulting room. Complex transference and countertransference issues between female therapists and women who kill are inevitable and require specialist supervision...

(Motz, 2008: 328)

Many perverse fantasies are mirrored in the relationship between FCSA perpetrators and female or even male therapists. Many female child sex offenders' past relationships have ended up becoming sexual; consequently, a transference relationship that erotises the therapeutic relationship is common, and many offending women interpret the therapist's non-sexual interventions as her wish to have sexual interaction with her (Saradjian, 1996).

Aiyegbusi writes about the dynamics within the staff, specifically nurses working in a secure female unit. She asserts how 'intolerable anxiety and fear are provoked in the patients, who anticipate the pain of rejection or perverse behaviour on the part of caregivers, based on the prior experience', prompting them to end the relationship. The care staff may not understand the women's internal perverse mechanism but may react with aggression, and thus, the original trauma is re-enacted (Aiyegbusi, 2004: 111). Aiyegbusi and Tuck add that 'at the very worst, the social environments of hospital wards and other hospital areas come to replicate the patients' internal worlds' (2008: 12).

Ruth felt that she needed to leave the evil inside the hospital – otherwise, she feared her world would end up being engulfed by it. The relevance of the secure unit's role is to contain within its walls the patients' memories and past and present pain, hidden as a defence against anxieties. When pain and memories are hidden, much is left to the imagination, including no evil existing outside the hospital gates (Motz, 2008).

Stolorow offers an intersubjective understanding of Ruth's terror about the evil taking over her world if she did not leave it behind the locked doors:

> Experiences of trauma become freeze-framed into an eternal present in which one remains forever trapped,…all duration collapses, past becomes present, and future loses all meaning other than endless repetition. Because trauma so profoundly alters the universal or shared structure of temporality, the traumatized person quite literally lives in another kind of reality. Torn from the communal fabric of being-in-time, trauma remains insulated from human dialogue.
>
> (Stolorow, 2008: 6)

Intellectually, Ruth understood her client; however, emotionally, she felt detached. Motz (2008: 352) asserts that being sentimental can propagate and camouflage violence. According to her (2008: 352), a sentimental 'attitude requires a suspension of objectivity or recognition of the conflicting qualities within the idealised person'. Kathy did not even attempt to be blinded by such an idealisation of her client, enabling her to think and feel amid therapeutic hardships.

Ruth was idealised by the staff and maybe even by her client. However, what would have ensued if she had created a string of emotional attachments by expressing sentimental emotions towards her client? I suspect that it would have proved immensely challenging working with Kathy's abusive sides, if not impossible.

Aiyegbusi (2004: 113) states, 'There is constant pressure to act out and when containment is not understood, and skills to think under fire have not been developed, then acting out by professionals is exactly what will happen'. The relevance of understanding the roles that are being projected onto the professionals by the patients is critical. This approach involves the professional deconstructing these projections before communicating them back to the client in a manageable form. It is through this process that the patient can learn more about themselves. Without understanding and processing the projections and the projective identifications, the re-enactment of trauma will continue to perpetuate.

How did the splits impact the therapeutic relationship? Ruth experienced Kathy as childlike, and she had to resist being lulled into believing the abuse never happened. Motz (2008) has recognised how, in many secure hospitals, female patients' rooms have stuffed animals thrown around. She believes that the staff infantilise adult patients as a defence against acknowledging the violence, sexual and otherwise, perpetrated by those women. In the case of Kathy, Ruth was aware of the dangers of infantilising her client and consciously resisted being lulled into seeing Kathy as a childlike figure.

The complexity of the therapeutic relationship is palpable. While Ruth felt she was being seduced into believing the abuse never happened, she also became entrenched in questioning her client's perpetrated abuse. These conflicting processes simultaneously took place within a determining context of suspension under the heel of her client's silence. Ruth's meaning-making of this dynamic is realising that she became, at times, like an abuser herself. Joseph (1985) and Sandler (1976) have demonstrated that patients' patterns of relating are enacted in the therapeutic relationship, and the therapist becomes part of that enactment. This point is also expressed in Stolorow's (2008: 2) statement: 'From an intersubjective-systems perspective, developmental trauma is viewed..., as an experience of unbearable affect. Furthermore, the intolerability of affect states can be grasped only in terms of the relational systems in which they are felt'.

Milton (2007: 189) outlines the problems of working with perverse female patients as follows:

> The therapist may become caught, as the patient is caught, in entrenched, repetitive patterns that feel inevitable, obvious, 'right' in some way, while at the same time indefinably uncomfortable or worrying.

Difficult dynamics demand self-aware responses from the therapist. Milton argues that the therapist needs to observe her responses and feelings honestly while also noticing her client's behaviour and emotions. The therapist may end up being reassuring, judgemental, and even patronising towards her patient who refuses to work with her.

> The strain and difficulty of this sort of work, and the honest self-scrutiny required, are part of the reason why intensive personal psychotherapy or analysis, and good supervision, are essential.
>
> (Milton, 2007: 189)

Ruth portrays a painful picture of Kathy being in a disorganised state and behaving like a toddler, unable to wash herself, bullying others, being bullied back, and then becoming a victim of this. Milton (2007: 189) asserts that women who have injured a child often have been hurt in their childhood by adults. To survive and take some control over their victimisation, they have erotised it, and their hatred and viciousness will be activated. She states that such a woman's internal object representations become cemented as brutal and punishing, requiring frequent acting out either in the role of the victim or a perpetrator.

Stolorow reminds us about the context of developmental trauma and the impact of 'a breakdown of the child-caregiver system of mutual regulation. This leads to the child's loss of affect-integrating capacity and thereby to an unbearable, overwhelmed, disorganized state' (Stolorow, 2008: 2).

The splits within societies are also easily observable. Welldon (2004) depicts a clear picture of the differences between how society regards FCSA offenders compared with male child sexual offenders. The same has been confirmed by Ford (2006), Motz (2008), Saradjian (1996), and many other clinicians.

Summary

This chapter is both an investigation into Ruth's working framework with FCSA, as well as an exploration of the possible impact posed by working with Kathy on Ruth's professional and personal life. Ruth found herself working within a web of unconscious and conscious defence/coping mechanisms that were manifesting as splits, both relationally and as a way of processing. I found a pathway through literary imagery to navigate, identify, and deconstruct these splits. In doing so, I sought to understand how Ruth processed the parallel manifestation of her emotional response system concerning working with Kathy. The application of both psychodynamic and intersubjective theoretical frameworks was used to broaden the perspectives involved in exploring FCSA. Furthermore, the discussions investigated how Ruth's specific vantage point, derived from her working experience, relates to and expands on the existing literature, which is universally deficient, particularly concerning the processes and dynamics between female therapists and female sex offenders.

The damaging impact of the denial of FCSA results in a failure to establish the necessary pathways needed to identify and address FCSA on multiple fronts, from policy intervention to cultural norms. On the one hand, services are inadequate or not developed to help victims and perpetrators. On the other hand, labelling women as evil prevents a serious engagement with FCSA. This culminates in reproducing further denial about the seriousness of female sexual abuse, as well as relegating and reinforcing FCSA as a behavioural outlier, separate from the normative definition and understanding of sexual abuse.

Bibliography

Aiyegbusi, A. (2004) 'Thinking under Fire: The Challenge for Forensic Mantal Health Nurses Working with Women in Secure Care', in Jeffcote, N. and Watson, T. (eds.) *Working Therapeutically with Women in Secure Mental Health Settings*. London: Jessica Kingsley Publishers, pp. 108–119.

Aiyegbusi, A. and Tuck, G. (2008) 'Caring amid victims and perpetrators: Trauma and forensic mental health nursing', in Gordon, J. and Kirtchuk, G. (eds.) *Psychic Assaults and Frightened Clinicians: Countertransference in Forensic Settings*. Forensic Psychotherapy Monograph series, Kahr, B. (ed.). London: Karnac, pp. 11–26.

American Psychological Association (2017). *Dictionary.com Unabridged*. Available at: https://www.dictionary.com/browse/split (Accessed: 13 December 2024).

Cartwright, M. (2017) *Scylla and Charybdis*. World History Encyclopedia. Available at: https://www.worldhistory.org/Scylla_and_Charybdis/ (Accessed: 12 December 2024).

Ford, H. (2006) *Women Who Sexually Abuse Children*. Chichester: John Wiley& Sons, Ltd.

Hinshelwood, R. and Skogstad, W. (2005) 'The dynamics of health care institutions', in Hinshelwood, R. and Skogstad, W. (eds.) *Observing Organisations: Anxiety, Defence and Culture in Health Care*. London: Routledge, pp. 3–17.

Joseph D. (1985) Humanism as a philosophy of Nursing. *Nursing Forum: An Independent Forum for Nursing*, 22(4), pp. 135–138.

Klein, M. ([1957] 1997) *Envy and Gratitude and Other Works, 1946–1963*. London: Vintage.

Lemma, A. (2004) 'On hopes tightrope: Reflections on the capacity for hope', in Levy, S. and Lemma, A. (eds.) *The Perversion of Loss: The Psychoanalytic Perspectives on Trauma*. London: Whurr, pp. 108–126.

Lemma, A. and Levy, S. (2004) 'The impact of trauma on the psyche: Internal and external processes', in Levy, S. and Lemma, A. (eds.) *The Perversion of Loss: The Psychoanalytic Perspectives on Trauma* (Series editors Fonagy, P. and Target, M.). London: Whurr, pp. 1–20.

Menzies, L. ([1959] 1988) *Containing Anxiety in Institutions. Selected Essays Volume 1*. London: Free Association Books.

Merriam-Webster.com Dictionary (2025) Available at https://www.merriam-webster.com/dictionary/lull (Accessed: 1 March 2025).

Milton, J. (2007) 'Technical problems in the psychotherapy of perverse female patients', in Welldon, E. and Van Velsen, C. (eds.) *A Practical Guide to Forensic Psychotherapy*. London: Jessica Kingsley Publishers, pp. 188–193.

Motz, A. (2008) *The Psychology of Female Violence: Crimes against the Body*. 2nd ed. London: Routledge.

Sandler, J. (1976) Countertransference and role-responsiveness. *International Review of Psycho-Analysis*, 3, pp. 43–47.

Saradjian, J. (1996) *Women Who Sexually Abuse Children: From Research to Clinical Practice*. Chichester: John Wiley & Sons.

Stolorow, R. (2008) The contextuality and existentiality of emotional trauma. *Psychoanalytic Dialogues*, 18(1), pp. 113–123. Available at: https://doi.org/10.1080/10481880701790133

Welldon, E. ([1988] 2004) *Mother, Madonna and Whore: The Idealization and Denigration of Motherhood*. London: Karnac. https://doi.org/10.1080/10481880701790133

Chapter 5

The breaking and making boundaries = the whirlpool feels like enmeshment

Introduction

The essential task of establishing and maintaining boundaries remains a foundational prerequisite as well as a perpetual challenge when working with FCSA. In the case of Ruth, it is evident that although the task is clear, the actual process of laying down boundaries is inherently porous to the relational dynamics emanating from Kathy. For Ruth, it was undoubtedly important to describe the specific pattern of Kathy's response to boundary-making. Kathy is described as exercising power through the deliberate and unconscious breaking of boundaries during the therapy, replicating the same pattern of behaviour which she had engaged in as a carer towards the children she was responsible for. These behavioural responses were rooted in Kathy's childhood. During her formative years, Kathy's perception of her reality had constantly been distorted by her parents lying to her, keeping secrets from her, and humiliating her. To her, there was no distinction between truths and lies; they became indistinguishable, comprising an entangled experience symptomatic of the wider trap of enmeshments. As a child, Kathy had not learned what 'no' and 'yes' meant. Her personal boundaries had not been respected, and as a result, she had not learned how to respect the boundaries of others. Ruth explores the importance of establishing boundaries during therapy so that both Kathy and Ruth gain a clear sense of the framework used and can strictly adhere to it, preventing re-enactments.

Breaking the boundaries

Ruth describes,

> I had one client who I worked with in the past... she committed sexual assaults on a small boy and small girls who she was taking care of in the role of a carer living in the house and so whilst she was in the house she ended up abusing the children that she was supposed to be caring for.

Ruth's client lived with a family, and her task as a nanny was to care for the children in their own home. Her professional role as a carer would have involved both physical

DOI: 10.4324/9781003607007-9

and psychological care with the overall objective of providing well-being and safety for the children. However, Kathy unequivocally broke the boundaries of her professional role when she invaded the children's bodies and minds. For me, this encapsulates an enmeshment in every sense of the word. No clear boundaries existed anymore; the children's protective skins had been pierced by sexual assaults. The abuser within Kathy relied on the camouflage offered by her role as a carer. The camouflage derived from her professional role engendered an indispensable duality in terms of utility that resulted in both the abuser role and the carer role being wholly dependent on the other, culminating in roles that became blurred and enmeshed. Both Kathy and the children became entangled in this landscape of dissonance and abuse delineated by the oscillating duality exercised and exploited through her performance of her professional role.

Ruth describes Kathy as having 'ended up' abusing children. There is a sense that Kathy had no other choice than to resort to abuse as if reacting to forces that existed outside the remit of her awareness. 'She was someone who had no boundaries, so she'd gone into a situation where she had control and power, and she had abused it'. It is evident that Kathy did not live her life within boundaries. She chose to go into a situation where she knew she had control over children whom she ended up abusing. However, she may have deceived herself into believing that she never intended to abuse them. Ruth says

that she enjoyed…I think this is the difficult bit that she enjoyed having the control, that she'd enjoyed having the power, that she'd sort of humiliated the children that she was caring for, she'd get them to dress up in all these clothes.

For Ruth, the mere thought of Kathy enjoying that control is difficult to process. Ruth depicts a terrifying picture of the little children having a dress-up game with their nanny without knowing that dressing up in 'all these clothes' was their nanny's way of sexually humiliating and controlling them. The dress-up games were planned by Kathy and were a clear example of how her abuse was orchestrated and not just an expression of her impulsive behaviour. It further substantiates the extent of power Kathy wields over the household: she is alone with these children and in full command.

About Kathy's formative years, Kathy's description of a stepfather was possibly a fantasy father figure, whilst her own father referred to her as a 'bastard', thus defining the very beginnings of her life as a curse. Her father used his parental role to humiliate Kathy, and she, in turn, used her role as a carer to abuse the children. Kathy learned to construct her own truths and lies to survive: no one helped or provided her with alternative ways of relating to the world. All conceivable boundaries were broken: carers became abusers; fantasy became reality; lies became the truth; the little baby became an unwanted bastard, and children became objects of control and sexual desire.

…she didn't know what the truth was. She said she had a stepfather, but he never existed, so I think it was this sort of mystical fantasy father figure that she never had, no one ever helped her, no one ever told her the truth, she had to lie, she'd be humiliated all through her childhood, and she said her father said once that she was a bastard.

Establishing and keeping the boundaries important

Establishing and maintaining the boundaries was imperative for Ruth when working with Kathy. Ruth had to be particularly alert to the more covert ways that Kathy would try to deploy to gain some proximity to children. It was clear that Ruth felt enormous anger about her client's seemingly deliberate plan to try to get her children's stories published. Even behind the secure doors of the prison, her client still tried to get closer to the children. Ruth elucidates, 'My initial reaction to whenever I heard that was, I was furious because she was trying to write children's stories, and she was trying to get them published, and we had to say "no"'. Although Kathy's attempts at reproducing some connection to children from prison could be described as more insidious, i.e., in the form of children's books, her objective to continue abusing was undeniably clear. What better way of gaining the trust of parents whilst capturing and occupying the imagination of children than through becoming an author of children's stories? Ruth's 'no' to Kathy's manipulation is short and firm despite her voice being whispery, and its message is clear for Ruth to take responsibility and stop the abuse.

> So, if I think of an example, she had a dummy, she came to the ward with a dummy, and one of the first things I said was you have to find more adult ways of comforting yourself, and so she ended up handing the dummy over.

Ruth was very firm in her approach with Kathy: no childlike comforting, no dummies, no regression, and staying in a childlike regressed position was allowed. A clear boundary was established: Kathy needed to find more adult-like ways to comfort herself. She needed to take responsibility for her behaviour, including looking after her needs. Ruth does not elaborate on whether it was difficult for Kathy to give up her dummy, but she did end up handing it over. This appears to represent a moment of progress as her dummy sucking also appeared rather perverse – a grown woman sucking a rubber object.

The team had to take responsibility by establishing firm boundaries surrounding protocol on family visits: not completing the sex offenders' treatment meant that no home visits were allowed. There was no room to take risks and be an irresponsible therapist. The boundaries were clear, and there were no 'ifs'. A safe place for Kathy, her family, and the staff had to be established. 'We have to be very careful about the family visits and I said there should be no family visits at all […] until she had completed the work, the sex offender treatment work'.

Discussion on the perspectives of breaking and making boundaries, and the felt enmeshment

The lack of boundaries and/or having a chaotic life, including their sexual behaviours, has often characterised female sexual offenders' lives (Ashfield et al., 2010). Women who have abused children sexually have had at least one relationship without boundaries with a child. They have also had their boundaries penetrated, and several had never had an attachment that had proper boundaries (Saradjian, 1996).

The paedophile creates perversion by twisting and manipulating reality by specifically denying differences between generations (Ruszczynski in Morgan and Ruszczynski, 2007). I have looked at a range of literature examining the perverse mother's use of their child as an extension of themselves (Glenn, 1984; Motz, 2008; Pines, 1993; Welldon, 2004). The child becomes an object of her mother, whom the mother can treat as she wishes without consideration of what the child feels and/or wants. The mother/career, who is supposed to nurture the child, uses the child for her pleasure and her own purposes. The boundaries are broken, and the child cannot escape the snare.

Ruth describes Kathy as enjoying having control over children when humiliating them. Lloyd-Owen brings understanding to trauma and control:

> ...if the trauma of abuse remains unprocessed and denied by themselves and significant others – either engage others in repeating the abuse, creating an illusion of control over the victim-role, or by turning passive into active, abuse others of an age and in circumstances to mirror their own original abuse.
>
> (Lloyd-Owen, 2007: 103)

Ruth had to work with and within the unknown and make meaning from Kathy's unknowns – what was the truth about her father/s, and were they only imaginary figures? During any phase of the child's development, the absence of a validating adult can affect the child's perceptions of, and formations of, her/his reality (Stolorow and Atwood, 1992). Shabad expresses the absence of validation of trauma as:

> In the absence of another person to validate the "event" of his suffering, the child is in the awkward, involuted position of proving the existence of his own experience. This places the person experiencing trauma in the position of the proverbial falling tree: "If there is no one to hear a tree fall in the forest, then did it fall?"
>
> (Shabad, 1997: 355)

One of the most fundamental components of trauma is that it blurs together perceived reality and fantasy (Nachmani, 1995). How does Ruth validate Kathy's existence? Ruth's account of her lived experience working with Kathy illustrates the importance of making meaning of Kathy's world without knowing certainly 'if the tree had even ever existed'.

When the boundaries are blurred, the roles are constantly exchanged, and any meaning-making becomes impossible. Nothing exists, but simultaneously, everything exists. Nothing ever happened, whilst everything has actually changed in that traumatic nothingness. To me, this feels like enmeshment.

The helpful definition of enmeshment for this study is given by Minuchin (1974), who introduced a notion of enmeshment referring to a family system in which there is an extreme form of closeness, and each family member is overinvolved in each other's lives. The boundaries in its subsystems become enmeshed, and children may take parental roles as there is no differentiation between subsystems. The enmeshment described by Minuchin can be seen in Kathy's life on various levels.

The team had to be firm and say 'no' to Kathy. When working with FCS perpetrators, the boundaries create a foundation for the women to have a sense of safety. Being directive in therapeutic encounters is essential and beneficial. These boundaries can be specific, depending on the legal status of these women, by defining, for example, the terms of visiting and contact with children. Moreover, the boundaries need to be defined individually depending on the needs of each woman: the woman might need to agree to have a contract on how to respect others by not verbally or physically abusing others or by using appropriate clothing (Ashfield et al., 2010).

Summary

Establishing boundaries is at the core of the therapeutic mandate, and Ruth upholds this in the strongest of terms with Kathy, remaining unwavering. However, the application of this mandate is not a foregone conclusion. Despite boundary-making being comprised of fixed, non-negotiable tenets, the process it undergoes is ultimately evolving and challenged by the immediate relational dynamics surrounding it. This chapter focuses on engaging with dissonant forces involved in establishing boundaries. The complexity is explored through the specific relationship between the boundaries broken by Kathy and those made and kept firm by Ruth to ensure that the abusive dynamics are not reproduced. Ruth's experience shows how, although boundary-making is a unilateral, top-down directive emanating from the professional mandate, her professional capacity to establish boundaries is not immune to the power dynamics stemming from Kathy. Kathy attempted to steer the configuration of the boundary-making process despite the clarity of the rules and the firm approach deployed by Ruth. In the case of Ruth and Kathy, Kathy engaged with Ruth's efforts in boundary-making through a sabotaging method of oscillation, mimicking learned patterns from her childhood and reproducing an entanglement of violation and adherence. Despite these sabotaging attempts, Ruth succeeds in maintaining the parameters of the boundaries, and Kathy handing over the dummy encapsulates this in a profoundly meaningful way.

Bibliography

Ashfield, S., Brotherston, S., Eldridge, H. and Elliott, I. (2010) 'Working with female sexual offenders: Therapeutic process issues', in Gannon, A. and Cortoni, F. (eds.) *Female Sexual Offenders: Theory, Assessment and Treatment*. Chichester: Wiley-Blackwell, pp. 161–180.

Glenn, J. (1984) Psychic trauma and masochism. *Journal of American Psychoanalytic Association*, 32(3), pp. 357–386.

Lloyd-Owen, D. (2007) 'Perverse females: Their unique psychopathology', in Morgan, D. and Ruszczynsky, S. (eds.) *Lecturers on Violence, Perversion and Delinquency*. The Portman Papers. London: Karnac Books, pp. 101–116.

Minuchin, S. (1974) *Families & Family Therapy*. London: Tavistock Publication Limited.

Motz, A. (2008) *The Psychology of Female Violence: Crimes against the Body*. 2nd ed. London: Routledge.

Nachmani, G. (1995) Trauma and ignorance. *Contemporary Psychoanalysis*, 31(3), pp. 423–450.

Pines, D. (1993) *A Woman's Unconscious Use of Her Body*. New Haven, CT: Yale University Press.

Ruszczynsky, S. (2007) 'The problem of certain psychic realities: Aggression and violence as perverse solutions', in Morgan, D. and Ruszczynski, S. (eds.) *Lectures on Violence, Perversion and Delinquency*. London: Karnac Books, pp. 23–42.

Saradjian, J. (1996) *Women Who Sexually Abuse Children: From Research to Clinical Practice*. Chichester: John Wiley & Sons.

Shabad, P. (1997) Trauma and innocence: From childhood to adulthood and back again. *Contemporary Psychoanalysis*, 33(3), 345–366. Available at: https://www.tandfonline.com/doi/abs/10.1080/00107530.1997.10746994

Stolorow, R. and Atwood, G. (1992) *Contexts of Being: The Intersubjective Foundations of Psychological Life*. Hillsdale, MI: The Analytic Press.

Welldon, E. ([1988] 2004) *Mother, Madonna and Whore: The Idealization and Denigration of Motherhood*. London: Karnac.

Chapter 6

Working process and progress = between the devil and the deep blue sea

Introduction

This chapter expands on the exploration of Ruth's therapeutic relationship with Kathy. The lived experience of Ruth's clinical working processes brings to light the following themes:

1 Struggles at the beginning

   Therapists who start working with FCSA may struggle to access and locate relevant sources of knowledge due to an underlying lack of supporting and informative literature on FCSA. The existing literature predominantly focuses on areas such as the characteristics of female sex offenders, explorations of their developmental years, and risk-related work issues. However, the production and availability of literature on the processes and dynamics existing between a female therapist and female sex offenders is severely limited.

2 Remembering the client's past trauma is important

   The necessity of the therapist remembering the client's past trauma as a prerequisite for making progress is explored. Ruth explores how remembering and engaging with her client's past aided in helping her better understand how the client had developed an identification with her primary abuser. The usefulness for her client of diary keeping and drawing a timeline to remember her past significant life events served as beneficial tools that enabled Kathy to connect more with her past.

3 Walking on ice = working with risk

   This theme highlights women's easier access to children than men. Ruth discusses her concern about her client's risky behaviour, her client acting out, and its impact on the therapeutic relationship. I find the imagery of ice helpful as it directly connotes the precariousness that lies in the fragility of therapeutic work. Therapeutic work can be described as walking on ice, which may crack at any time, causing Ruth and her client to fall into deep and murky waters.

4 Circumvention of the complexity of therapeutic work is not an option

   Therapeutic work is a must. The difficulties of working with the presentation of child-like and deviant traits simultaneously occurring in the same person are

DOI: 10.4324/9781003607007-10

explored. The significance of her client gaining a more coherent sense of self by drawing links between her behaviour, past trauma, and deeper awareness of the consequences of her actions is stressed. In this section, Ruth also movingly describes her emotional and intellectual responses to her client. Furthermore, the section looks at how her client denied her abusive behaviour and impulses.

5 Importance of the team/supervision

The importance of the role of the team, coupled with external supervision and the importance of writing notes, is stressed and explored.

Struggles at the beginning

I think at the beginning I found it very difficult because you never read very much about it and there's not very much in the literature…it was quite strange, and it felt quite uncomfortable, I was almost out of my depth when I started working with her.

These words expressed by Ruth illustrate how the genesis of a therapist's journey working with FCSA may feel. Ruth's words point to an overriding systemic deficiency in the production of knowledge related to FCSA. This epistemic deficiency is evident both within the domain of professional work as well as at the societal level. On the whole, access to information on FCSA is not widely available through various cultural outlets, with FCSA receiving scarce attention in the media. Whilst trying to find her words, Ruth says that she had felt uncomfortable and strange as she initially waded her way through this mostly concealed landscape. Her initial struggles are expressed through the idiom 'out of my depth' which refers to 'not having the knowledge, experience, or skills to deal with a particular subject or situation'; 'in water that is so deep that it goes over your head when you are standing' (Cambridge Dictionary, 2025a: no page). Although Ruth was standing, the water submerged her head: seeing, hearing, and thinking were almost impossible.

'…you know a particular profile which you don't necessarily feel the same with women'. Ruth's reflection underscores a systemic assumption, namely that female offenders fit the same profile as traditionally known profiles of sex offenders. A therapist who has worked with male offenders might struggle to work with female offenders if maintaining the same therapeutic approach. Ruth asserts that therapy with female offenders needs to be more individual-based than with males.

'She was a very difficult person to work with…, I think people struggled to work with her because of what she had done, I was very aware of how other people were about her'. Ruth pauses whilst talking about the difficulties of working with this client. These pauses seem to capture her broader struggles and challenges in her work. She was also aware of the difficulties her other hospital team members had with her client because of what she had done.

I found it difficult with her because connecting with her as a person was quite difficult. It was very strange, and I think because she tried to deny talking about the abuse for a long time, she categorically refused to talk about it.

The difficulties that Ruth faced in establishing therapeutic rapport with Kathy appeared at the very outset of their work. Despite Ruth articulating that connecting with Kathy as a 'person' was difficult, she does not suggest that it would be preferable not to connect with her client. For Ruth, Kathy was not a specimen to be mechanically observed. Being able to connect with her was key in establishing a successful therapeutic working relationship, which required both emotional and intellectual understanding. The experience for Ruth was not only one that she had never encountered before, but it was also made even more challenging due to Kathy's refusal to talk about the abuse she had perpetrated. This refusal, instigated by Kathy, ended up becoming a determining obstacle to Ruth's main therapeutic objective. The therapeutic relationship became stuck: Ruth would try to make her client talk whilst Kathy remained unflinching in her silence. These extreme positions were established from the beginning of the therapy.

Remembering the client's past trauma is important

'She had ended up in that situation because of her own trauma of being abused'. Ruth alludes to her client sexually abusing children because of her own experience. 'And so, to me then, often at those very difficult times, I would go back and just think why this woman has ended up in this way'. Remembering and contextualising Kathy within her history of trauma and its devastating impacts sustained Ruth when she encountered challenging moments with her work. Recalling Kathy's past seemed to have given Ruth a deeper vision and an understanding that propelled her to keep going when there didn't seem to be much hope to break free from the impasse. Furthermore, understanding her past trauma seemed to have helped Ruth obtain a non-judgemental position about her client's perpetrated abuse.

> What I found helpful was thinking about this person from a psychodynamic perspective. What helped was thinking about how she had identified with her abuser, and for me this helped formulate how her difficulties developed in childhood and the same of those relationships being re-enacted in the present.

Ruth's decision to apply a psychodynamic approach with Kathy demonstrates how the application of psychodynamic perspectives helped to engender alternative, non-polarising ways of interpreting her behaviour. Understanding the part of Kathy that identified with her abuser helped Ruth to locate how her client's difficulties originated in her childhood, and how re-enactments of those relationships kept perpetuating. Being able to identify Kathy's present behaviours as a re-enactment enabled Ruth to see beyond her client's behaviour and reach out to her client with greater empathy. Ruth's empathy towards her client comes across as being inextricably linked with her understanding of Kathy's past. It is precisely because of this that she can navigate with care her client's past trauma, her perpetrated abuse, and her present and past abusive patterns towards herself and others. Empathy is unequivocally the determining factor in the success of the therapeutic work, yet as earlier established, it has to exist within firm boundaries. I explore this type of empathy in further detail in Chapter 10, *Bold empathy*.

'She had her own book to write things down, and then she would look back at the book in the week. We did things like a timeline with significant events in her life, and that helped her connect more'. This citation exemplifies how, by linking the past and the present, Kathy was able to connect with herself. This included feeling less judgemental towards herself, whilst gaining further meaning and understanding of her behaviour. Furthermore, through a process of writing down significant events, Kathy was able to reflect more deeply. Spoken words became written words, these words were further developed and formed, and the process provided her with added help and self-understanding.

> And it was about trying to think about what those initial slides made her feel quite small, weak, and vulnerable, and how difficult it was for her to sit with that because it made her feel like when she was younger.

Ruth needed to help Kathy recognise and process the initial moment that had brutally wounded her, consequently resulting in her becoming an offender. The meaning of 'slide' for me here is 'the process of moving into a worse state, often through lack of control or care' (Cambridge Dictionary, 2025b: no page). Children slide down the slide in the playground. The mudslides down the hill, covering everything underneath. Kathy, as a child, slid into being abused; she had no control over stopping it.

Because of the various meanings of the word 'slide', one could also see how a child could perceive what the perpetrator does as a playful act until the mud of abuse slides on the child and covers everything in its secrecy. Therapy created a space where Kathy was able to revisit her childhood experiences of feeling small and vulnerable; however, staying with those feelings was hard for her: remembering meant connecting. Yet, within that space of remembering, Kathy was not alone; she was guided by Ruth. Being provided with anchoring, in the form of Ruth, ensured that Kathy did not have to end up being dragged further down with the vast, powerful whirlpool of childhood re-enactments. Nevertheless, despite the presence of this anchoring, there was an incessant threat of the all-consuming whirlpool.

Walking on ice = working with risk/safety

'I never felt she really took her offending seriously, and I felt I wouldn't know when she had because you never knew when she was being honest or when she was not'. Ruth's words demonstrate that no assurances existed when it came to instilling trust in Kathy's words. There was no way for her to ascertain whether her client had realised the seriousness of what she had done. The relationship and work were not based on trust: the meaning and intention behind Kathy's words were often unknown. The therapy sessions with Kathy can be described as 'walking on ice': she could never know whether the ice was breaking or whether they would ultimately fall into what lay underneath: the deep and dark waters of the more unknown.

> She did things like going on a bus and being near children or the school up the road, I felt more worried about her as a woman than I did about a man because I thought there are so many ways that women can have more access to children.

Ruth's observation regarding Kathy's female identity serving as a form of camouflage for her perpetrating confirms the default bias present in the societal perception of women. In other words, by virtue of being a woman, Kathy would not be seen as an obvious threat and would therefore be allowed access to children. This was a serious concern for Ruth. Kathy is portrayed as walking near schools, travelling by bus, and being near children. She is part of our everyday scenario; she is among us. Kathy, a woman, is interested in children: she wants to care for them, write stories, and draw pictures. The fear is that this interest masks and is interspersed with sexual and controlling feelings about them.

It was evident that Ruth was very concerned about her client's choices and behaviour, as she says,

> On a professional level, it was concerning because here was someone who deliberately ended up putting themselves in a situation where they had access to children, then abused that power, then denied any responsibility and still refusing to accept any responsibility,…who had done all this but sort of minimising and blaming the victims they had led her on sexually to do it…from a risk point of view, it was very concerning.

This excerpt describes her client's offending profile: her deliberate choices to gain access to children, the abuse of her power, her constant denial of any responsibility for her perpetrated abuse, her minimising the abuse, and at times blaming the children for seducing her. Although Ruth recognised that Kathy's pattern of behaviour had largely become rooted in her psyche, she also believed that a part of her client's behaviour was chosen and that the unremitting risk of re-offending was always possible. Ruth's deductions reinforce that the potential for re-offending is amplified due to a fixed societal bias that ascribes women as being inherently incapable of offending.

> She'd wear a Minnie Mouse T-shirt when she went on leave, and so, of course, children would come up to her…she used every conceivable possibility…and I thought, is she consciously doing this? Am I being paranoid? Am I being hyper-vigilant and just thinking here is someone who's going out deliberately targeting, grooming, and overcompensating for the fact that people aren't worried where she's going…but what was worrying was that children would come up to her…, even though she was a woman in her thirties, there was something quite emotionally underdeveloped about her.

The scenario described by Ruth of Kathy wearing a Minnie Mouse T-shirt conjures a female child-like Pied Piper leading and grooming children through her infantile demeanour. Was she deliberately grooming them, or was she dressing in this child-like way, as she intrinsically identified with the children themselves? This question perturbed Ruth and led her to wonder whether she had become irrationally suspicious. Ruth's experience of doubting herself connotes a parallel picture of an abused child questioning their rightful instinctive and intuitive processes. Those who encounter the Pied Piper end up questioning their sanity and, at the same time, becoming further entrapped inside the cave. Ruth could identify and deconstruct the mask of the Pied Piper. Yet whilst utilising this insight, she was simultaneously aware of the vast extent to which this mask goes unnoticed within society. The work triggered many conflicting and difficult feelings in Ruth; at times, she doubted her sanity. It is evident that therapeutic work situated between danger and safety affects the therapist in significant ways.

> It felt like if things like that weren't dealt with directly, there'd be a danger... there were so many levels of things that were going on that I had to grasp and try and deal with and hopefully by taking one concrete thing away we could work on the other issues.

This extract powerfully depicts how the threat of 'danger' can easily arise if the therapist is overwhelmed and unable to address pressing issues. One can see the therapist almost drowning under the multiple tasks. Ruth does not finish her sentence when talking about ignoring the danger. Would finishing her thoughts be too frightening? Ruth had to deal with one issue at a time, knowing that there were numerous issues to be dealt with. Many issues are concrete, and some therapists learn in their training to pay attention only to internal reality. Based on Ruth's voiced experience, it becomes clear to me that when working with FCSA, the work exists between an interplay of imagined danger and the possibility of children becoming sexually abused in reality.

How does one work with such issues and clients? The next sub-theme will explore how the therapists navigate the challenges stemming from the conflicting space between imagined and real threat and how the perpetual risk of recidivism is a grave concern.

Circumvention of the complexity of therapeutic work not an option

> I'd got quite stuck with her... Stuck in the sense...you know there was work that had to be done but she refused to acknowledge she had problems or any issues, and I just felt like I was saying, this needs to be done...

I think this extract reveals the difficulty and tension comprising the act of responsibility. Who is fundamentally doing the worrying? Ruth or Kathy? Who is acknowledging the abuse and the dangers? Kathy must do it, but Ruth is never sure she does, yet her future risk reduction depends on it. An impasse ensues.

'I tried to get her to think about what her self-harming was doing for her, and it was often about punishing herself for her offending…She was able to start talking about the offending'. Here, the importance of helping the client to formulate her thoughts and feelings is accentuated. Getting Kathy to start thinking and talking about her self-harm, as well as linking it to punishing herself for offending, opened the door for Kathy to introduce the subject of perpetrating abuse.

> How difficult it was for her to have so much control and power and not to know what to do with it…I think this is the difficult bit that she enjoyed having the control and the power, that she'd sort of humiliated the children that she was caring for. She'd get them to dress up in all these clothes and that was…the sadistic side of herself…to think about the parallels in the present where she deliberately disclosed her offence to people who were traumatised, and had been sexually abused so she could see them unravel and have power over them… it was difficult not to feel revulsion, to be honest…What I found difficult was how she would target the vulnerable and the needy, and that made me feel very angry, and it was a lot to hold to stay professional in those moments.

In Ruth's view, for Kathy to have power was very difficult, as she did not know what to do with it; she misused it by harming the children she cared for by involving them in sadistic games. In therapy, Ruth had power over her client by establishing and keeping rules and boundaries. This was not abusive power, yet I wonder how this form of power was interpreted in her client's mind and whether any boundary felt punitive.

There are several keywords in this extract, such as 'power', 'control', 'offending', 'humiliating the children that she was caring for', 'sadistic side of herself', and 'self-harm'. These keywords, together with the expression 'she'd get them to dress up in all these clothes' for her perverse enjoyment, seem to shout out the word danger. Kathy enjoyed having power and seeing people unravel and go to pieces. The therapy helped her to draw parallels between her sexual offences and disclosing her offences to people on the ward, many of whom had been sexually abused in childhood. Kathy also revealed her childhood sexual trauma by re-enacting it through her abusive actions.

Ruth felt revulsion seeing her client enjoying wielding control. Thinking about her client targeting the vulnerable evoked feelings of anger in Ruth and proved testing to 'stay professional' during those times. What does Ruth mean by 'staying professional?' She says:

> It was hard to keep those two extremes in mind, and I didn't kind of agree with either of them. She was such a complex person. I think I probably jumped at times from one to another extreme, because she was very needy, very desperate for help, very desperate for any sort of attention.

It was essential for Ruth to draw on her understanding of Kathy's complexity: her neediness and desperation for help, while remembering her very cruel and even sadistic sides. Nevertheless, Ruth acknowledges that at times she jumped between those extreme sides.

> To try and get her to take responsibility and to become more adult-like, she was very keen to stay in this childlike, no responsibility…I mean, in a very perverse, weird state she was happy in, I wanted to get her into a healthier, more functional state…I tried to get her to explore what her behaviours were doing for her, and what their function was. Could she see herself living like this in the future? Try to encourage her to develop more adult ways of being, and that there could be benefits of being more emotionally robust and responsible than kind of cheating into this very childlike way of interacting.

Ruth tried to get Kathy to take responsibility for her ways of behaving and not staying child-like. There is a sense that Ruth worked strenuously in getting Kathy to engage more by challenging her: what her behaviour was doing to her, and whether she wanted to continue living in this way. The significance of communicating hope that change was possible was created by encouraging Kathy to develop more adult ways of being.

> I was trying to understand what the function was, why she was doing this? And why is she putting some of these feelings into me as well? Who is this anger directed at? What is this anger about? She never got angry at the people who had abused her.

Anger was a central issue during the therapy. What was the function and the meaning of her anger? Ruth almost comes across as a detective-like figure trying to get to the depth of her client's anger by asking why, what, and who. The anger was also felt by Ruth: some of which was her own anger, and some of which she experienced as being put into her by Kathy. Coexisting with Kathy's expression of anger was the reality that Kathy had never been able to be angry at her abusers. The extremes are evident: Ruth's anger, Ruth's feelings of Kathy's anger, and Kathy's lack of anger towards her abuser. Ruth had to be able to contain those extremes in her mind.

> I was trying to help her with her anger. And because she found it very difficult to express her anger or any frustration, someone would upset her, and she would bottle it and wait for months until she could get that person on their own, and then insult them quite badly. It was essential to get her to work with that and resolve tiny conflicts without letting them escalate so that her only two options were either physically attacking them badly or psychologically attacking by revealing her offence. We drew out this volcano and we thought about how, and that seemed to connect with her better, but I found out that I worked more eclectically with her.

Kathy's anger was like a contained volcano that inevitably would explode. The hospital team worked on helping Kathy to be able to express her anger as well as resolving even small tensions. The team drew the 'anger volcano' out. In other words, they worked actively together and helped Kathy learn alternative ways of dealing with her wrath rather than violently harming others and herself.

> We ended up being quite creative, and she had her own book, and what she'd find helpful was to write down in the sessions what we'd talk about. She'd often bring that to the session, an incident on the ward that happened that week, and we'd often try to get her to think and understand the process of what happened, get her to connect with her feelings because that's something she'd always struggled to do. She'd say, "Oh yeah, I felt like self-harming, so I self-harmed", and there was never really any kind of emotional connection. So, trying to slow it down and get her to think about her feelings, name them, think about how other people might feel, and start to think about the alternatives.

Ruth and the team tried to help Kathy think about alternative ways of being: slowing down, thinking about her behaviour and feelings, connecting with them, naming and understanding her processes of what had happened/was happening in her life. Additionally, they tried to help her develop her relational capacity by exploring other people's feelings and to gain some empathy towards others.

'Even though the interventions were very boundary-basic...helping her to understand that maybe there was more than one way of being, she found it quite empowering'. This process has a sense of togetherness: the team working together with Kathy fostered a process that was empowering. This task of working together further aided in preventing splits from occurring within the team.

We did things like a timeline with significant events in her life. That helped her connect more, she seemed to work better when there was a focus and not when we just sat in a room and there was nothing, no material. Ruth used some therapeutic tools outside of the verbal relationship; one of these tools was a timeline when working with Kathy, which helped her to feel focused and connected. The timeline seemed to represent a grounding reference point offering some certainty and structure, whilst lessening feelings of the unknown and nothingness she harboured inside.

> I was the one saying we need to focus on this, and it made me more aware that I had to be so careful not to get drawn into these very perverse relationship patterns with her, that we had to stay equal, and it would be far too easy for me to slip into that person that's doing all the questioning and becoming abusive.

There is a sense of must here being exercised by Ruth. Ruth appears unequivocal in utilising her awareness of refusing to partake in a perverse, sado-masochistic relationship as she describes. Ruth's actions strongly substantiate the critical need to challenge the existing denial of the repetition of abusive relationships through a process of self-awareness and intersubjective equality. The importance of not letting things go unnoticed was imperative for Ruth. She repelled any potential for the repetition of adopting roles that were not caring and that did not name the unnamed. It was clear to Ruth that this would only validate and normalise Kathy's pre-existing history of clandestine, unhealthy, and perverse relationships.

> But at the same time, it was easy for her to coast and not connect with anything, which was exactly what happened with her abuse. It just went unnoticed, and no one cared. I had to be much more self-aware when working with her because of the nature of her relationships. She was only used to unhealthy, toxic, perverse relationships, so I had to be very careful that I didn't get drawn into doing that.

Kathy had learnt to exist without making any relational effort, nor connecting with anyone during her abuse. Ruth did not want this norm for Kathy to be repeated in therapy. Ruth does not elaborate further on what staying equal means, but she articulates that she needed to avoid getting into sado-masochistic relationships with Kathy. It was Ruth's responsibility not only to stay equal and to acknowledge the powerful pull behind the abusive patterns, but also to resist the attempted coercion, Kathy's unconscious invitation, willing her to become a partner in that abusive game. Ruth had to maintain clarity regarding these extreme opposites: the work being a must; her client retaining a stance of being passive, while Ruth was positioned as the one responsible for getting the work done, whilst simultaneously staying equal.

Ruth relied on psychodynamic thinking to understand her complex client.

> My relationship with my supervisor helped me to think of her in a much more psychodynamically informed way because she wasn't robust enough to work in that manner. It had to be on a very here-and-now cognitive basis. I felt the different strands helped me, and probably the cognitive side helped her to stay focused.

Despite Ruth finding a psychodynamic framework supportive when trying to understand Kathy, Ruth acknowledges that her client was not strong enough to do psychodynamic work. Ruth did not push her client to fit into one therapeutic model. Moreover, it was the cognitive approach that helped Kathy to focus and work on her present issues. The overriding aim of the therapeutic work was not centred on an in-depth exploration of Kathy's childhood trauma but rather on how she had perpetrated the sexual abuse and how she was still engaging in repeating the abusive patterns.

Importance of the team/supervision

'Over time, it was supervision that helped me go through it. I used to write process notes. We used to have lots of team meetings. I had external supervision as well, which I found helpful'. Contemplating Ruth's words, 'getting through', there is a palpable sense that she experienced the work as difficult. Ruth needed to detoxify her mind and would outsource her thoughts and feelings about her work through writing. Supervision provided her a sense of containment and connection; she was not working on her own. Furthermore, attending external supervision, as well as frequent team meetings that integrate the work within the team, reveals Ruth's indispensable need to have a support system in addition to having an external thinking space, to be able to manage the complex nature of the work.

'I brought the case to peer supervision, talked about my work, and people who weren't directly involved helped see things from different perspectives'. It was essential for Ruth to reflect on her work through different angles and to engage with people who were not directly involved with her client and who were able to help Ruth deal with this difficult work. The distance helped them to see the blind spots and explore the case more objectively.

'With the team, I tried to think quite systematically about how to work with her, and think about the impact she has on everyone because she did affect everyone, and it helped...' The word 'systematically' refers to thorough explorations and reflections. Kathy greatly impacted all the people on the ward. Identifying and studying the influence that Kathy exerted over the team members reinforced Ruth's work by enabling her to incorporate this specific insight into her understanding of Kathy's relationship patterns and dynamics.

'I started working a lot more with the nurses as well and just thinking about how we can get her to be more resilient, more self-aware, and just on the most basic levels...' The collective effort through working with the team is stressed again. There had to be clear communication and understanding among the team members on how to work together. Prompting Kathy to become more resilient, so that she would be able to both withstand difficulties and recover from them, was one of the main priorities of the work. The expectation was that in becoming resilient and more self-aware Kathy's risk of re-offending would be reduced. Ruth did not try to do the work on her own but valued working together with the team. The team seemed to reach a stage where they were able to integrate the split aspects of Kathy, which had been projected onto the different team members.

Discussion

The genesis of Ruth's work with Kathy was characterised by struggles and anxieties. Concerning reducing the anxieties of staff who work with forensic patients in closed institutions, Welldon (2007: 17) asserts:

> Setting and surroundings are important...Institutions should provide structures to protect the therapists from inherent anxiety produced by working with forensic patients. If the diagnostician is not well trained, a new confrontation could easily be experienced by the prospective patient as a further condemnation of his/her illegal action.

While Ruth was well-trained and made great efforts to provide structure and communication channels among her team members, there was a lack of literature to support her, which rendered the work more difficult. Organisations need to ensure that their staff are provided with information and support on how to enable female survivors to manage the impact of their trauma. I believe that the same need also exists for female sex offenders. Aiyegbusi (2004) states that if there is no framework for staff to adhere to when working within a female secure unit, conflicts, including envy and toxic communication, will consequently build up between the staff members, making it difficult to care for the patients.

The significance of having a gender-specific approach for the benefit of female offenders and clinicians is rightly emphasised and should not be overlooked. Ruth struggled in the beginning to work with females who did not fit into the male offender model. Ashfield et al. (2010: 166) assert: 'It is equally important to consider the impact of sex socialisation not only concerning clients' responses but also practitioners' responses'.

It was important for Ruth to remember and make meaning from the driving forces that had brought Kathy into this situation. One way of validating the client's experienced past trauma is by containing it. This requires the therapist to remember and to keep the client's trauma and its construction in mind. Garland (2004: 110) explores the process of the baby taking in the mother's milk as 'the mother's capacity to tolerate and manage anxiety – her own and her baby's'. She links this to Bion's ideas of describing transformations as a process, that what a mother can do to the baby, the therapist can do to the client – to help the client to hold in mind and think about what had been considered before to be unbearable.

The therapist, by remembering and acknowledging the client's trauma, validates not only the client's traumatic experience but also her being. Validation of trauma, according to Levy, 'refers to the therapist's acknowledgment of the patient's actual experience and not simply the internal state of the patient' (Levy, 2004: 52). Levy refers to working with torture survivors: 'The validation of a survivor's experience is probably the most containing therapeutic gesture a therapist can make...' (Levy, 2004: 53). Trauma is experienced as the trauma of something distressing and harrowing. Levy clarifies that the 'what' needs to be acknowledged and not just the 'how'. This is further explored in Chapter 7 *Do we see? Do we hear?*.

Ruth understood Kathy was identifying with her childhood abuser, and this vital step helped Ruth to understand how her client had ended up as a perpetrator. Ruth seemed to have made sense of her client's position as the perpetrator, similar to Lemma and Levy's (2004: 13) explanation of what the losses experienced by the survivor of trauma evoke: '...an experience of the event rather than memories of what is lost. It is as if something concrete has been forcibly installed in the mind, abrogating attachment and replacing it with a new aggressive identification. This can be understood as an identification with the perpetrator'. This is not to say that all female sex offenders have been sexually abused as children.

Ruth and the team worked with the constant fear and awareness of Kathy being at risk of re-offending. The dynamic risk factors of female sex offenders don't seem to be fully known, and hence, Cortoni (2010) argues that the potential risk for recidivism must be based on components that seem to be common among female offenders and their offending behaviour: some features of female sex offenders are suggested to be similar to the male offenders' behaviour. Both tend to deny and minimise their offending behaviour and show distorted cognitions relating to how they perceive it. They use sex as a regulation for their emotional states and to satisfy their need for intimacy. Female sex offending is also associated with humiliation and sexual gratification. Relationships and intimacy are also problematic. Correction Services Canada and Lucy Faithfull Foundation (LFF) have formulated structured and gender-based treatment approaches that are mainly cognitive behavioural and focus on helping sexually offending women to challenge their cognitive distortions. However, LFF has also integrated treatments such as schema therapy, dialectic therapy, and trauma therapy into their approach (Blanchette and Taylor, 2010).

Ashfield et al. (2010) recommend that therapists give homework that includes achievable goals to the woman, which she agrees to do. Reaching her own goals gives her a sense of achievement and additionally motivates her to work towards further goals. They emphasise the importance of practitioners being flexible and adapting their styles of working to each individual's needs. The need to be flexible is firmly confirmed by Ruth's therapeutic approach, too.

The issues of assessing risks of re-offending are beyond the scope of this chapter. In any case, risk assessment is complex, and the therapist must take into consideration whether the woman offended on her own or with someone else, as well as her possible criminal background, her family history, and her past possible victimisations. The woman's sexual fantasies, thoughts, and behaviour need to be looked at, among other issues (Cortoni, 2010).

Ruth makes clear that therapeutic work is 'a must' and not an option. The work entails many aspects. One of the main tasks is to recognise the female offender's survival tactics, and how they function to fulfil their felt and vital needs (Eldridge and Saradjian, 2010). Ruth talks about how she experienced her client defending herself by self-harming. Kathy humiliated others and enjoyed the sadistic effects of her actions while enjoying having power over others and seeing how they unravelled under her power. The therapist must make meaning out of those defences together with her client.

Self-harm, according to Motz, communicates the idea that 'women harm themselves primarily to express their distress and anger' while wishing that others will notice and respond. They externalise their internalised pain, direct their rage, and attack the self to lessen their inner pain (Motz, 2008:197). The women may also attack 'their own identity as mothers or potential mothers symbolising the dangers inherent in sexual relations' (Motz, 2008: 201).

Motz also elaborates how a victim of sexual abuse experiences her body as 'the split-off body', and in her self-preservation attacks her 'bad' self so that her 'good' part of the body can be situated above the violence and survive. Sometimes, the victim feels the need to punish herself for her false belief of inviting the abuse to happen (Motz, 2008: 198–199).

In the case of Kathy, she attacked her body through self-harming, and it was Ruth's task to make sense of those defences and to help her deconstruct and process her inflicted self-harm. The transference relationships formed by the self-harming client's unconscious needs mustn't be seen as a hindrance to treatment but rather as a way to understand the patient's internal world. The aim is to help the patient verbalise and articulate her pain and manage it without enacting it by injuring herself (Motz, 2008).

Providing the client with a safe place to regain her sense of being through verbalising her emotional experiences is a central aspect of the work, as Stolorow points out in his definition of ontological unconsciousness:

> Linguistically, somatic affectivity, and attuned relationality are constitutive aspects of the integrative process through which the sense of being takes form. The aborting of this process, the disarticulation of emotional experience, brings a diminution or even loss of the sense of being…a hallmark of the experience of emotional trauma. The loss and regaining of the sense of being,…hinging on whether the intersubjective systems that constitute one's living prohibit or welcome the coming into language of one's emotional experiences.
>
> (Stolorow, 2008: 4)

Kathy did not only injure herself but also others through humiliating and sadistic behaviour. Ruszczynski states: 'The *sadistic* act…seeks to torment and control the feared other whose emotional reaction is crucial: the specific aim is to cause the object to suffer, physically or mentally' (Ruszczynski, 2007: 30). The sadist must have some understanding of the victim's mental state to know what causes the victim to suffer.

The link between being a victim and a perpetrator is also identified by Aiyegbusi (2004). Women in secure units are not just targeting themselves with self-harm, but they also make others suffer. The roles of being victim and perpetrator of suffering are exchanged all the time: 'The need to make others suffer may be a strategy for managing unprocessed pain… that cannot be thought about' (Aiyegbusi, 2004: 112).

There are several other key aspects. Matthews (1998) in Gannon and Cortini (2010) identified that FCSA offenders need to experience empathic responses to develop empathy towards others . Ruth's empathy was built through the process of understanding, and throughout therapy, Kathy's understanding of herself also increased. This point is confirmed by Stolorow (2008: 3): 'Only when her analyst became established as an attuned, understanding presence could these symptoms begin to become transformed into nameable terror'.

During the sessions, some homework was used to help the client to focus. The empty and unknown space was filled with something concrete. The importance of using homework has also been asserted by Ashfield et al. (2010). Ruth's experience of Kathy was that she tried to soothe her anxieties in the same way a child would soothe herself. So, Ruth helped her client by using homework to find more adult-like self-soothing behaviours.

When interviewing female sexual perpetrators, Saradjian (1996) found that women felt that they were in control and had power during sexual activity with children. Otherwise, they felt they had less control over their own lives than other people, including children. Ford (2010: 108) states that some women only experience physical closeness when there is a power imbalance, and that female sexual offenders 'may therefore have a number of interpersonal difficulties for consideration in treatment'.

Saradjian (1996) found that not one female perpetrator, at the time that they were actively abusing children, could name even one friend. Likewise, Ford (2010) refers to Strickland's (2008 in Ford, 2010) comparison of female sexual and non-sexual offenders on the Social and Inadequacies Subscale, which found that the sex offenders had more difficulties in their social and sexual contacts than the other female offenders. These theoretical frameworks provide some understanding and links to the problems experienced by Ruth's client while living in the hospital community and her difficulties in connecting with others.

Ruth needed to ensure that she had all the necessary support to work with Kathy efficiently. The provision of supervision should create a safe space for an examination of the therapeutic relationship and the therapist's motivations and interventions. Saradjian (1996: 215) points out: 'The importance of good honest supervision for all casework cannot be stressed enough'. Ruth found the support derived from those who were not directly involved with her work to be very helpful.

Conclusion

When therapists lack the very specific knowledge related to working with FCA offenders, they are likely to feel submerged by the deep waters as Ruth did. As challenging and as difficult as it might sound, the therapists resiliently work their way through the waters, rising and breaking through the icy surface of the therapeutic relationship. Therapeutic work becomes a challenging process in which clients' past traumatic experiences and volatile relationships hide in the dark waters, yet the clients' behaviours, feelings, and relationships are visible, almost tangible beneath the thin, fragile barrier of ice. For therapists, remembering clients' past traumas, perpetrated abuse, and present actions is critical. Engaging with the past trauma gives them a broader understanding and a deeper empathy, which are necessary to navigate through the cracks in the therapeutic relationship whilst acknowledging their existence and developing mechanisms through which to better deal with them. Both team and supervisory support become invaluable in empowering therapists to cope with the struggles they face with difficult clients and to provide quality services. It must also be said that the critical importance of gender-specific therapy when working with FCSA offenders cannot be overemphasised.

Bibliography

Aiyegbusi, A. (2004) 'Thinking under Fire: The Challenge for Forensic Mental Health Nurses Working with Women in Secure Care', in Jeffcote, N. and Watson, T. (eds.) *Working Therapeutically with Women in Secure Mental Health Settings*. London: Jessica Kingsley Publishers, pp. 108–119.

Ashfield, S., Brotherston, S., Eldridge, H. and Elliott, I. (2010) 'Working with female sexual offenders: Therapeutic process issues', in Gannon, A. and Cortoni, F. (eds.) *Female Sexual Offenders: Theory, Assessment and Treatment.* Chichester: Wiley-Blackwell, pp. 161–180.

Blanchette, K. and Taylor, K.J. (2010) 'A review of treatment initiatives for female sexual offenders', in Gannon, A. and Cortoni, F. (eds.) *Female Sexual Offenders: Theory, Assessment and Treatment.* Chichester: Wiley-Blackwell, pp. 119–141.

Cambridge Dictionary (2025a) Cambridge University Press and Assessment. Available at: https://dictionary.cambridge.org/dictionary/english/out-of-depth (Accessed: 23 February 2025).

Cambridge Dictionary (2025b) Cambridge University Press and Assessment. Available at: https://dictionary.cambridge.org/dictionary/english/slide (Accessed: 09 January 2025).

Cortoni, F. (2010) 'The assessment of female sexual offenders', in Gannon, A. and Cortoni, F. (eds.) *Female Sexual Offenders: Theory, Assessment and Treatment.* Chichester: Wiley-Blackwell, pp. 87–100.

Eldridge, H. and Saradjian, J. (2010) 'Replacing the function of abusive behaviors for the offender; remaking relapse prevention in working with women who sexually abuse children', in Laws, R., Hudson, S. and Ward, T. (eds.) *Remaking Relapse Prevention with Sex Offenders: A Sourcebook.* London: Sage Publications, Inc, pp. 402–426.

Ford, H. (2010) 'The treatment needs of female offenders', in Gannon, A. and Cortoni, F. (eds.) *Female Sexual Offenders: Theory, Assessment and Treatment.* Chichester: Wiley-Blackwell, pp. 101–117.

Garland, A. (ed.) (2004) *Understanding Trauma: A Psychoanalytical Approach.* London: Karnac Books.

Lemma, A. and Levy, S. (2004) 'The impact of trauma on the psyche: Internal and external processes', in Levy, S. and Lemma, A. (eds.) *The Perversion of Loss: The Psychoanalytic Perspectives on Trauma* (Series editors Fonagy, P. and Target, M.). London: Whurr, pp. 1–20.

Levy, S. (2004) 'Containment and validation: Working with survivors of trauma', in. Levy, S. and Lemma, A. (eds.) *The Perversion of Loss.* London: Whurr Publishers, pp. 50–70.

Motz, A. (2008) *The Psychology of Female Violence; Crimes against the Body.* 2nd ed. London: Routledge.

Saradjian, J. (1996) *Women Who Sexually Abuse Children: From Research to Clinical Practice.* Chichester: John Wiley & Sons.

Stolorow, R. (2008) The contextuality and existentiality of emotional trauma. *Psychoanalytic Dialogues,* 18(1), pp.113–123. Available at: https://doi.org/10.1080/10481880701790133.

Ruszczynsky, S. (2007) 'The problem of certain psychic realities: Aggression and violence as perverse solutions', in Morgan, D. and Ruszczynski, S. (eds.) *Lectures on Violence, Perversion and Delinquency.* London: Karnac Books, pp. 23–42.

Welldon, E. (2007) 'Forensic psychotherapy the practical approach', in Welldon, E. and Van Velsen, F. (eds.) *A Practical Guide to Forensic Psychotherapy.* London: Jessica Kingsley Publishers, pp. 13–19.

Section 2

Horror and sorrow

Requires compassion and understanding

Introduction

The agonising and pervasive impact of F-to-FCSA, visible and non-visible, on those affected is relentless in its grasp, very often lasting a lifetime. Many victims end up living a life that is inundated with unspeakable horror and sorrow. There is no doubt that the response to this requires a resounding extension of compassion and understanding. Despite the sequential colossal and universal suffering, there remains widespread denial of FCSA within society, including the field of psychotherapy. The presentations in this section attempt to put forward these two sides of F-to-FCSA: the horror and sorrow on the one hand, and the need for compassion and understanding on the other.

Section 2 is divided into three chapters

1   Chapter 7: Do we see? Do we hear?
2   Chapter 8: The mind-blowing venom of the FCSA
3   Chapter 9: Many faces, many levels

Before progressing further into the chapters, it is important to introduce the five therapists, Linda, Helen, Greta, Mary, and Sarah, whose clinical experience is central to this section. In addition to each therapist offering their own unique perspective, all five therapists gave insightful, intimate, and useful accounts, providing comprehensive knowledge of their clinical experiences. Their experiences are integral to this chapter. Let me introduce them one by one.

Helen, a warm and friendly middle-aged woman exuding a no-nonsense attitude, is a psychotherapist in both private and prison settings. She started her work with sex offenders as a probation officer 30 years ago, specialising in working in prison settings and establishing programmes for male sex offender groups while also working with individual female sex offenders. Helen compared her work with female offenders to male offenders and explored the link between female offenders' emotional neediness and their offending. She also examined how her work with offenders had changed over the years and stressed the importance of having an individual and gender-specific approach, which includes exploring clients' past traumas and not just their offences.

DOI: 10.4324/9781003607007-11

Linda talked about society's denial of the existence of FCSA and how it has changed over the last 40 years. Her work experience has included the exploration of the vulnerabilities of women concerning pregnancy and childbirth. Linda also talked about intergenerational abuse and emphasised that therapists need to suspend their emotions to be able to do this work. Although she did not discuss in great depth how the work had affected her personally, she did open a window revealing the tears she carried for those women whose children had been taken away, as help had arrived too late.

Greta, a warm middle-aged woman and a qualified psychotherapist, talked about her work with a female victim of FCSA, the first one she had ever worked with. Compared with the other participants, she had the shortest working experience, equating to two years. From this angle, her specific viewpoint as someone working for the first time with FCSA provides a rich and significant contribution to the complexities of working with F-to-FCSA. Greta stressed the importance of being honest and congruent with one's clients; however, there was also a sense of hesitation in exploring her own struggles.

Mary, a middle-aged woman, is a clinical psychologist; she has 35 years of experience working with both male and female survivors of FCSA. Mary, a survivor of MCSA herself, spoke movingly about what had aided her journey of recovery. Her client knew about Mary's trauma, and through Mary's voice, one can hear points of convergence, where they met, as the therapist and as the client: the two survivors.

Sarah, also a middle-aged woman, has a vast track record of working within prisons, the National Health Service, the courts, the private sector, as well as being an author. She has worked with female sex offenders and their victims for about 30 years. Her emphasis was on the importance of creating a shared language: without listening, there is no hearing. Sarah is a fighter, and her voice is an embodied voice calling for gender equality for female offenders and their victims.

Chapter 7

Do we see? Do we hear?

Introduction

The denial of the existence of FSCA can be identified throughout various domains, from societal attitudes to the core of the therapeutic work setting. Although Linda specifically explores how women are predominantly perceived as not being capable of sexually abusing children, she also recognises some increased awareness of this phenomenon. For Sarah, there exists an urgency in calling for professionals to realise that FCSA exists. Mary navigates her way through the mind-blowing FCSA incidents behind the drawn curtains. Greta's description is at odds with the others in that she describes meeting her client's alters, which are primarily seen as concealing the abuse. Helen reflects on the varying ways in which society and the courts treat female offenders differently from male offenders.

Mary and Greta, as well as Helen and Linda at times, describe their clients' trauma histories and 'how' doing therapy cannot happen without knowing and acknowledging the 'what'. This trajectory comprises the main context and essence of the work as the 'what' and 'how' are intertwined and inseparable. The portrayed picture of the 'what' is seen as being fluid, its 'colours' changing all the time, yet it matters.

The presentation in this chapter focuses on the following themes:

a The impact of the denial of FCSA on services
b Nice women do not sexually abuse
c As if it never happened
d Camouflaging the abuse
e Making sense of society's complex view of FCSA

The impact of the denial of FCSA on services

Linda:

> Because of the lack of acknowledgment, we cannot offer any resources, and the perpetuation of the abuse is not being acknowledged in the first place. The only way one can make any changes is to acknowledge and improve your

DOI: 10.4324/9781003607007-12

understanding of this, but if one doesn't acknowledge, one can imagine that the problem doesn't exist…it is far more frequent than what we'd expect, as we always want to believe in motherhood's sanctity.

Linda states decisively that society's non-acknowledgement of the existence of FCSA prolongs the cycle of abuse. According to Linda, the non-willingness to acknowledge FCSA stems from the fundamental belief that motherhood is sacred, and therefore, there is a concerted effort to preserve this essence of purity to protect our sanity. Motherhood is upheld by many in society as existing above normal humanity, in some ways sanctifying it as untouchable. Linda contends that the first step must be to accept its existence; if we cannot acknowledge it, then there is nothing to be understood and, as a result, nothing to be changed in terms of how we treat perpetrators and victims of FCSA.

Nice women do not sexually abuse

Sarah: 'In a training event, we were talking about someone working within a faith setting and the difficulties that they are experiencing with people simply saying – but nice women don't do that'. In Sarah's experience, there is a lot of denial and/or minimising of the existence of FCSA. For example, individuals within some faith backgrounds refuse to believe that ostensibly nice women can abuse children. People see their front-stage behaviour and refuse to believe that any sinister activities could exist underneath that surface.

Sarah continues:

> We will get comments like 'she's just over affectionate' or 'she's just got boundary issues' or 'it's not abuse because she didn't mean to abuse.' This makes professionals feel less uncomfortable but masks the reality of the abusive behaviour and the experience of it for the children and the victims.

Sarah's observations demonstrate how the denial and impact of FCSA is not solely confined to the parameters of society; it is, in fact, visibly operating among professionals. To provide a more palatable rationale and to mitigate the discomfort and anxiety that professionals experience when working with FCSA, they resort to making excuses for the woman's abusive behaviour, to the extent of re-naming it. This masks the perpetrators' abusive behaviour and denies the validity of the victims' experience. That endemic denial seems to stem from a parallel process of engaging with denial between the offenders and the therapists, and consequently, nobody takes the victim seriously.

As if it never happened

Mary:

> It was a very dirty house. When social services would visit, the parents wouldn't open the curtains, pretending they were out. One thing they used to

do was bury her alive. What Ann, the youngest of the female children, also did, which I can relate to in my own recovery, was to keep her mind intact by distancing her mother from the abuse, as if she wasn't actively involved when in fact she was.

Ann's childhood was contaminated not only with physical dirt but also with the denial of her parents, her community, and the social services overseeing her and her siblings. The pain of Ann and her siblings was ignored. The curtains were drawn, obscuring visibility between those who should have seen and those who were hiding: the perpetrators. Who ultimately benefitted from that barrier, the abusers, and/or the seers? Whose responsibility was it to remove those 'curtains'? In Ann's childhood, there was no transparency, and it seems that by Mary listening, hearing, and re-telling Ann's trauma, she chose to be the seer: the transparent therapist.

As Mary says, what 'they used to do was bury her alive'. Being buried alive evokes the image of Ann being the actual dirt that was deemed necessary to get rid of; it further evokes an image of Ann being somewhat dead but also alive. To be imprisoned with no certainty as to whether you will live or die and to be buried by one's own mother, suffocating from the dark heaviness of the earth, the lack of air, and isolation, were all beyond any doubt insufferable experiences. Yet the question surfaces, was it safer for Ann to be under the ground than to be in the presence of her mother and other abusers? How could Ann survive it, then and now? Mary connects the outcome of Ann being buried with Ann intentionally burying and distancing herself from experiencing her mother as an abuser. Ann's symbolic burial of her abuser-mother, who is alive, is concealed under the earth of denial. The symbolic burial was necessary for her mind to remain intact. To be buried = to be safe from splitting apart – to keep the mother figure away from being an abuser = keeping her mind intact. This seems to point towards the lack of separation between Ann and her mother, as if feeling rage towards her mother and seeing her mother as an abuser would destroy Ann's sanity. Mary compares Ann's behaviour of burying as a coping mechanism utilised to keep her mind safe within her very own recovery processes.

There is a sense that the therapy between Ann and Mary could be seen as a form of 'un-burying'. What will be revealed when the soil is removed and the curtains are pulled? No memorial stones to mark her grave: her half-dead, half-alive little body momentarily freed from being actively sexually abused, whilst her resurrection would inevitably bring her back to being abused. Could the therapy be a part of laying down stones on her grave, signifying the space between dissociation and not knowing, giving a voice to Ann's story?

Mary:

I don't think that we should necessarily throw away the key because this is what was told to me. I had post-natal depression and psychosis after giving birth. A lot of my experiences came back, and I was very young when I had my first child, so I was put through the psychiatric system and pumped with a lot of drugs.

Mary openly describes her experience of managing to cope with the painful trauma of being sexually abused by her mother. Her trauma was masked under post-traumatic depression and psychoses, and her body was pumped up with medications. She says that many incidents that had been hidden came back to her memories.

Camouflaging the abuse

Greta says: 'Starting in the bath being told how unclean she is and how she's got to be cleaned and washed, filthy and evil, so yeah I don't think it gets much worse than that'. Greta is deeply affected by her client's trauma and believes nothing could get worse than that. Her client's mother camouflaged her perpetrated sexual harm by telling her daughter that she was the wicked and the dirty one, and her dirtiness had to be washed away.

She adds: 'Sometimes it comes out in one of her alters, and it turns to herself, so she regularly self-harms, except most of the time she's not aware – but when she cuts, she comes back to the present'. In Greta's experience, her client felt anger through her alters and turned it towards her 'corrupted' self. Her client's mother had disguised the abuse, and at times her client would repeat this behaviour of concealing by disguising the impact of the trauma. However, as Greta asserts, self-harm helped to prevent her client from becoming dissociated and, in fact, resulted in bringing her back to the presence of her body. She re-enacted elements of the abuse by her mother; however, the trigger and the outcome of the self-harm departed from the original experience of her mother's abuse, in the sense that her behaviour stemmed from a survival impetus, producing an aliveness of dissociation. Out of the six therapists I interviewed, Greta is the only one who described her client as having 'alters', sometimes taking over her personality. For me, Greta's client's ways of coping are like another form of the F-to-FCSA – octopus arms penetrating.

Making sense of society's complex view of FCSA

Helen's words:

> That attitude judges make a lot of excuses for women. Sometimes, when women are picked up with men, the men go to prison, and the women get probation or a community order. Probation officers make sure, it depends if it's a woman on her own without a guy, like working in the nursery school, she is going to bite the dust big time because of all sorts of other factors. Judges want to reassure the public that nurseries are safe. There's still ambivalence and two minds about women, how can women do this, and no resources are put in.

During her 30 years of working with sex offenders, Helen experienced the existence of ambivalence regarding the punishment of female sex offenders. On one hand, female offenders working within the education system get long punishments;

on the other hand, some co-offending women might get probation, unlike their male partners, who go to prison. The judges and other officials seem to either minimise their crimes by finding excuses or heavily judge these women, leading to no effort to offer resources to help them. Helen continues: 'The women can't see a way out, and if we could allow these women to feel safer and come forward'. Helen calls for a change in society where offending women would feel safer, not monstrous, and as a result would come forward and seek help. Reforming the denigrating cultural representation of female offenders would hopefully reduce the continuation of the abuse cycle.

Discussion

When writing this chapter, I saw a bleeding wound of F-to-FCSA being secretly and poisonously further aggravated. The wound throbs, and the poison contaminates the victim's and the perpetrator's bodies and minds, spreading to the other family members, inevitably trickling down through the generations. The impacts are mind-blowing: A shameful festering wound that needs to be covered is produced. Those affected are hindered from thinking and processing, ultimately feeling powerless to reach out for help. The inflicted find a way of coping with the wound that knows no bounds, sometimes even pretending it does not exist.

The word 'wound' derives from the Greek word *titrosko* – to pierce, which refers to trauma, a mark resulting from the piercing of the skin. *Titrosko* originates from the verb *teiro*, having two meanings in ancient Greek: to rub in and to rub off/away. Therefore, it can be extrapolated that the word 'wound' suggests two opposite movements (Papadopoulos, 2002). One can see how those two opposite movements of *teiro* meet in the therapeutic space between all five therapists and their clients. The rubbing-in is explored in this chapter, and the rubbing off/away will be investigated in the chapters *Many faces, many levels* and *Bold empathy*.

All the interviewed therapists voice the critical importance of exploring 'what happened to the client'. The piercing, the first movement of *teiro*, the rubbing in, that produced the wound matters, and the wound itself matters, too. Sarah, Linda, Helen, and Mary voice their collective experience, asserting that society and many professionals have difficulties acknowledging the survivors' and perpetrators' pain and that this type of trauma impacts everyone touched by it, including professionals.

During one of my psychotherapy trainings, I was presented with rather simplistic views about choices and freedom. In a presentation of Sartre's philosophical views of choices, one lecturer claimed that we were always free to choose our perspectives on what happens to us. This would include our past experiences. I asked the lecturer how he regarded a baby or a child who had been sexually abused, making choices concerning their experienced abuse, and the answer I received was that they could make a choice later in life on how they viewed the abuse. This meant that it would be the victims' responsibility to: (i) decide how they viewed the sexual abuse experience, and (ii) how they process the emotions and their level of impact on them, varying on their perception of the incident/s and their contexts. To me, this perspective seemed to put an enormous burden on the victim, as choosing to call the trauma abuse would also mean choosing to carry the pain.

Another lecturer of mine claimed that CSA is a cultural construction. Treating CSA as a cultural construction as well as the abuse of a vulnerable infant who has no choice for the sexual gratification of an adult are both unequivocally wrong. The views expressed by these two lecturers make me think that some psychotherapy lecturers have adopted Foucault's view that the perception of having or not having sex with children is only a cultural construction. Foucault formulated his view, claiming that Victorian aristocracy confined sexuality in their own home to protect their inherited virtues and control the lower classes through the Christian churches' teachings of shame. However, this was demystified by Sears (2023) as an illusion. According to her, there were several societal movements during the Victorian period fighting against the slavery of women and children in brothels. A large demonstration of 250,000 people in Trafalgar Square demonstrated against the buying of a child for prostitution, prompting the issuing of a bill, the Criminal Law Amendment Act of 1885, which raised the age of consent for girls from 13 to 16. Sears (2024) reveals further the very concerning fact that teaching paedophilia as an acceptable form of sex has spread to some psychotherapy teachings through the ideas of Foucault and Rubin, a follower of Foucault. Rubin, in her paper 'Thinking sex', adopted Foucault's previous claims about Victorian sexual oppression and promoted Foucault's ideas of paedophilia and cross-generational sex as normal.

Concerning the importance of exploring past abuse memories in the therapeutic sessions, some approaches may say that they are unnecessary or even harmful. To gain more understanding, I provide a brief exploration of what the literature says about trauma memories and their importance to therapy. The question is, are trauma memories no more than just hazy reminiscences that we can easily ignore?

Several researchers have regarded early juvenile memory recollections as being re-constructed later in life to divulge personal truths instead of objective facts (Mitchell and Morse, 1998). In the therapeutic process of the client talking about their life experiences, their story develops into a purposeful 'narrative' not intended to present the past as facts (Mitchell and Morse, 1998). However, psychotherapy may offer a 'narrative truth' – a consistent understanding of a person's history that helps the client and the therapist understand the client's present sufferings. Therapists must remind themselves of the importance of believing clients' experiences while remembering that some of the clients' memories might not be accurate. Allen (1991) suggests that validating the client's present experience is a necessity for the client to make sense of her past and present experiences in therapy sessions. Lemma (2016) postulates that for the client's narrative truth – the construction of the past – to be healing, the therapists need to view it as genuine as one would regard historical facts. As a therapist, we can only support the client's emotional understanding of their past and their narrative of it.

Bowlby states: 'Ever since Freud made his famous, and in my view disastrous, volte-face in 1897…it has been extremely unfashionable to attribute psychopathology to real-life experiences' and that therapists should accept their client's stories as being estimates of the truth (Bowlby, 1988: 87). Not validating the clients' experiences would not be therapeutic. For the interviewed therapists, it was clear that their clients tried to make sense of their past and present experiences by telling their stories, and that the therapists attempted to make sense of their clients' experiences and the impact of this on the therapeutic work.

A MCSA survivor whom I interviewed for my MA, whose trauma had not been validated, told me:

> …not having it acknowledged that I was abused by the professionals from whom I sought help…being forced (by my therapist) to reconnect with my mother as a condition of therapy…I had seen many therapists since I was twenty-one and none of them had told me that I had been abused…it would have helped me to hear it sooner rather than have to learn about it on my own from books.
>
> (Getu, 2003)

The above extract strongly conveys how the therapist didn't seem to listen to her client's narrative, nor did she connect with her emotions to better understand the client's core pain and how sexual abuse perpetrated by her client's mother had immensely impacted her client's life. Instead, the therapist forcefully and harmfully asked her client to reconnect with her perpetrator-mother as a pre-condition for the therapy. A question arises from this citation: should we tell the clients that they have been abused if they or we suspect that? Is that the validation that they need to receive? This question became a major issue in the therapeutic work with the client I worked with several years ago. At the beginning of the therapy sessions, it emerged that one of her previous therapists had told her that she had been sexually abused by her step-maternal uncle. That therapy had been a six-session therapy that she had received through the National Health Care. The client had no memories of being sexually abused but experienced lots of physical and emotional sensations that could be related to childhood trauma, including being sexually abused. No memories had returned to her during the sessions despite several therapists having used various approaches, including somatic experiencing and alternative approaches such as rebirthing and scream therapy in their practices.

Quite soon after the start of the therapy, an issue surfaced. She wanted me to tell her that she had been sexually abused, and I could not give that confirmation to her. We faced an impasse several times during our therapeutic relationship as the client felt I didn't validate her trauma of being sexually abused, whilst I could not ethically make such a statement. The client made huge progress in numerous areas of her life, such as discontinuing to regress to a childlike person rocking and hugging her teddy bears and dolls soothingly in the sessions, and retaining her excrement. She often felt angry towards me because I would not 'diagnose' her as sexually abused. During those times, I was viewed by her as if I were her abuser who refused to admit to her the perpetrated sexual abuse. It also seemed as if she viewed my position as having built a coalition with her mind's limitations. It felt as if her mind and I had potentially failed her for refusing to allow her to remember her past assumed memories of abuse. She also projected onto me her stepmother, whom she feared to initiate discussions about the assumed abuse, while also raging against her stepmother for not confirming that it had happened. During these times, she would express her wish to find the therapist who had given her that original affirmation. The therapist from her past had come to represent the good object in my client's mind, capable of healing her, while I was the bad object keeping her away from recovery by withholding an abuse 'diagnoses'. During those angry sessions, I started to feel powerless and less convinced that any significant change could occur. The therapy was at an impasse despite working through her issues from various perspectives and staying with her pain on several levels. A therapeutic breakthrough was set in motion when the client began to grieve the experience of not knowing if she had been sexually abused. Instead of feeling powerless, I felt strong empathy towards her as a person, her anger, sense of helplessness, and grief. I reflected afterwards and wondered if I experienced a powerful countertransference or an intersubjective experience, as it seemed to happen within the client and me at the same time. I continued to embrace and validate fully her narrative story, including her anger towards me and herself, which she was able to receive. The deadlock was released. The client was able to move on in her life and make remarkable changes regarding her living circumstances, work, and relationships. The therapist's task is to help the client bear the anxiety of their unknown by bearing their own anxiety of the client's unknown. Yet, we need to validate and listen to the client's narrative about the trauma events as they are revealed to them (Lemma, 2016).

Adshead (Adshead and Horne, 2022), a psychotherapist who has worked extensively in secure psychiatric hospitals with people who have killed when mentally ill, has developed the concept of 'radical empathy'. She explains that the word 'radical' derives from the Latin *radix* root, as the aim of the therapy is to look into the client's past. The therapist, together with the client, explores the traumatic memories. The therapist must remember the offences and consequences of their clients and keep hope while unravelling the complex emotions and past life experiences to help them take responsibility for their violent acts to reduce the risk of reoffending. Adshead explores how she uses the concept of 'radical empathy' in action in her book *The Devil You Know* (Adshead and Horne, 2022).

It is generally advised that therapists should not explore the exact details of the incidents of abuse. However, for Mary, Greta, Helen, and Linda, it was important to describe some of the details of their clients' experienced trauma. I also assume that the clients described the traumatic stories of their own accord to the extent that, for example, Linda and Mary emphasised being blank canvases during the sessions.

Up to this point, I have referred to the denial of FCSA taking place within both the societal and therapeutic domains. However, it seems that even some clients deny it. Greta brings to the fore a diverse picture of her client, denying and suppressing the abuse within herself, by splitting into various personalities to protect herself from the experience and aftermath of the horrific abuse. During some sessions, the alters felt safe enough to appear and voice their existence. The defence mechanisms employed by some survivors of incest comprise innate splitting, denial, and dissociation. Dissociative identity disorder (DID) often stems from ritual abuse in which 'alters' form in response to severe trauma. Multiple personalities are constructed with dissociated identities and behaviours (Mollon, 2002; Sinason, 2002). However, due to the limitations of this book, DID will not be explored further.

I want to finish this discussion with a court case of a paedophile ring in Glasgow (O'Hare and Renton, 2025), describing a paedophile ring of seven perpetrators, including two women and five men who brutally physically, psychologically, and sexually assaulted children, including boys and girls. The children had been registered under the Glasgow City Council since July 2018. However, it took almost two years to stop the abuse and for the horrendous crimes to come to light. During the court, the jury heard how the little girl as a toddler was frequently raped by the paedophile ring members. One girl had been put in an oven, locked in a cold fridge, put in a freezer, and repeatedly locked in a cupboard and made to eat dog food and nailed to the kitchen wall by her clothes to hang there for ten minutes. Children had been given drugs, turning their worlds into bizarre and eerie places. There had also been allegations of witchcraft, but they had been withdrawn. I see the colossal similarities between the above-described case and what Mary and Greta describe in this chapter. The Glasgow case is a stark reminder that no one who has awareness should turn a blind eye to any form of child sexual abuse; turning a blind eye becomes synonymous with being an active participant in it.

Summary

In this chapter, the impact that stems from the denial of the existence of FCSA and the myriad ways in which it affects society, including prison services, therapeutic treatments, and sometimes even training institutes, is brought to the fore. The insidious ways in which FCSA hides inside the victim, by the victim unconsciously engaging in various defence mechanisms, are probed. This chapter also investigates how clients' memories and their narratives are indispensable and must be validated by their therapist. Whilst the narratives of the victims' and perpetrators' past cannot be regarded as absolute objective truths, the pivotal significance of listening and validating the narratives is emphasised. How to work with memories of abuse or the lack of them in therapeutic settings is also explored.

Bibliography

Adshead, G. and Horne, E. (2022) *The Devil You Know: Encounters in Forensic Psychiatry.* London: Faber.

Allen, C. (1991) *Women and Men Who Sexually Abuse Children: A Comparative Analysis.* Brandon: The Safer Society Press.

Bowlby, J. (1988) *A Secure Base*. London: Routledge.

Garland, C. (ed.) (2004). *Understanding Trauma: A Psychoanalytical Approach*. London: Karnac Books.

Getu, L. (2003) *An Exploration of Female-to-Female Child Sexual Abuse*. MA thesis, City University.

Lemma, A. (2016) *Introduction to the Practice of Psychoanalytic Psychotherapy*. 2nd ed. West Sussex: Wiley Blackwell.

Mitchell, J. and Morse, J. (1998) *From Victims to Survivors: Reclaimed Voices of Women Sexually Abused in Childhood by Females*. Washington, DC: Accelerated Development.

Mollon, P. (2002) 'Dark dimensions of multiple personality', in Sinason, V. (ed.) *Attachment, Trauma and Multiplicity: Working with Dissociative Identity Disorder*. Hove: Brunner-Routledge, pp. 177–192.

O'Hare, P. and Renton, C. (2025) How victims shone a light on 'beastly house' child abuse ring. *BBC News*. Available at: https://www.bbc.co.uk/news/articles/c2ld7enjj9eo (Accessed: 14 May 2025).

Papadopoulos, R. (2002) *Therapeutic Care for Refugees: No Place Like Home*. London: Karnac Books.

Sears, T. (2023) Debunking myths about Victorian sexuality. *Hermeneutic Circular*, pp. 26–29.

Sears, T. (2024) Against queer theory. *Hermeneutic Circular*, pp. 11–15.

Sinason, V. (ed.) (2002) *Attachment, Trauma and Multiplicity: Working with Dissociative Identity Disorder*. Hove: Brunner-Routledge, pp. 177–192.

Chapter 8

The mind-blowing venom of the FCSA

Introduction

This chapter probes into the causative transgenerational cycle of sexual abuse, having special focus on abusive mothering as an embodied mind-blowing trauma which blows one's mind away to the extent that the mind stops thinking. It is the physical and emotional violence that predominantly lies behind the offenders' cycles of abuse. The portrayal of female child sex offenders as victimised, vulnerable, passive, and trapped whilst actively abusing is intimately portrayed. The tangible impact of the venom of FCSA on the offenders and the victims is explored. This chapter depicts the poison of FCSA being rubbed into the vulnerable victim's wound as it camouflages, hides, poisons, and causes blindness, whilst both the survivor and the perpetrator are powerfully affected to the extent of the possibility of their psychic self-destruction. The victims' and perpetrators' painful experiences described have a direct impact on the therapeutic relationship.

The themes covered in this chapter include the following:

a   The abusive mothering – the embodied mind-blowing trauma
b   Penetrating and reaching all over – knowing the 'what'
c   The transgenerational cycle of abuse
d   The Nakedness of Eve the Perpetrator: victimised, vulnerable, passive, and active

The abusive mothering – the embodied mind-blowing trauma

Mary says the following: 'The first person who gives birth to you abuses you. I mean, that's something I still work on in my own recovery. If your mother can reject you but also actively abuses you, it is really mind-blowing'. Out of all the participants, it is Mary who can understand how mind-blowing MCSA can be, having been sexually abused by her mother and still in recovery. In her experience, it blows one's mind away to the extent that the mind stops thinking.

DOI: 10.4324/9781003607007-13

Mary reveals:

> With client Ann, the sexual abuse happened independently of the stepfather. The mother was single for a while, and client Ann was abused from her earliest memory – maybe two until the age of four. Fondling then became painful, implements were used vaginally or anally, and this caused Ann a lot of pain, and how it affected her psyche. It was difficult to hear such a lovely girl hating the way she looked, she was naturally a beautiful girl and such a gentle soul. She would pull her hair out and try to disfigure herself because she thought that all men wanted was her looks, as she was also abused by the stepfather and the paedophile ring.

For Mary, it was an unbearable experience to hear Ann's narrative and to feel the hideous trauma wounds being rubbed into Mary's client's body/mind as well as the therapeutic relationship.

Mary's lived experience of Ann's traumatic past: Ann had been sexually, physically, and emotionally abused by her mother and others, all of whom had shown no consideration for her. Mary represented the antithesis of this dark backdrop of personalities; she seemed maternal towards Ann, admiring her sensitive soul and beauty. There is no sense of sexuality in Mary's expressions: she admires Ann as any mother would admire her daughter. Ann hated herself/her looks, and by disfiguring herself, she wanted to eliminate the 'badness', as if her looks were the cause of the abuse. Although not explored by Mary, it seems that for Ann to be seen by Mary as beautiful inside-out was an immensely humanising, yet at the same time frightening experience. More importantly, there is a sense that through Mary's humanising lens, Ann was potentially able to distinguish a humanising form of admiration, separate from the paedophiles' abusive usage of her beauty to serve their narcissistic consumption.

Penetrating and reaching all over: knowing the 'what'

This is Greta's voice:

> The mother took her to ritualistic abuse from the age of twenty months old in another house daily, where she was handed to a satanic cult, where she witnessed babies being killed. She was forced to drink blood and participate in many sexual acts involving people and implements. Although the mother was a conduit through which the child was forced into these satanic rituals, it transpired in the flashbacks and dreams that the mother sexually abused as well.

Greta continued describing the heinous sexual acts perpetrated by her client's mother on her daughter. I have chosen to omit the depictions as they are too horrible and could be traumatising to read. Greta says: 'The truth is always what appears to be the truth at that time because the truth can change and that's okay, that's not lying, that's truth changing by recollections and memories'.

The total powerlessness of the little girl who was contaminated inside-out, physically, sexually, and visually, is portrayed by Greta. The blood she had to drink would not only 'nourish' but also poison her body as a symbol of life and death; therefore, there was an undeniable and tangible enmeshment between the forces of life and death. How could anybody survive such experiences, and what would surviving mean? I wonder how Greta could sit in the room face-to-face with her client and listen to the most revolting things her client had experienced. The reader and the listener also become voyeurs to the most painful acts done by a mother to her daughter. When writing this, everything in me felt repulsed, and I wondered whether Greta felt the same repulsion. Greta's battle with the traumatic experience of her client resembled to me an *octopus* – wide-reaching, camouflaging, penetrating, venomous, and alive. It kept shifting invariably, reaching out with its arms into every part of the therapy.

Undoubtedly, the therapeutic relationship was intensely impacted by her client's story, which fundamentally informed the therapeutic work. However, I ponder why Greta talked about the horror with such detailed, graphic words. Greta's words seem to accentuate the viewpoint that there was no 'how' to work with the client without 'what'. This was specifically evident with Greta's client, who experienced multiple parts, namely that the ever-changing 'what' is part of the 'how'. The therapeutic work takes place within that constant fluidity and uncertainty.

Greta's working experience was quite limited at the time of seeing her client, and I had wondered whether that had played a role in her being so descriptive about the trauma. Did the trauma incidents become more highlighted due to the lack of long-term working experience? Or could I say the opposite, that due to her lack of extended working practice, she had not yet developed any inhibitions regarding talking about her client's pain so openly?

During the interview, I did not detect any erotic countertransference in Greta's voice and manner towards her client. However, I do take into consideration that Greta's descriptive words could be interpreted as her expression of being impacted by an erotic transference felt by her client towards her. Yet, it is important to state that there is no evidence of her client experiencing such a transference, other than the inevitable confusion of a sexually abused patient faced with a maternal transference figure, and for that reason, the concept of erotic transference is considered in the discussion section of this chapter.

The transgenerational cycle of abuse

Linda:

> I had a patient, for example, a mother who had five children…, I interviewed the mother, who said she preferred to masturbate her children than to give them the dummy, because they go to sleep, and they sleep much better because when her husband comes, he is very abusive to her. Now, she used to abuse all the children, and one of the children, her daughter, is one of the patients I have seen

for treatment for years. She was referred because she had a problem with exhibitionism, and that exhibitionist behaviour took place in the doctor's consulting rooms. She would come to the consulting rooms, and the same strategy would happen. She would be ready with the clothes, go into a room, to make little noise, and then when people are looking just to open all her dress, or sort of a big zip, or a lot of buttons, to show her completely naked underneath and then everybody would be very shocked, and she would disappear.

Linda describes transgenerational abuse as experienced by her patient: a mother sexually abusing her children and then, later, her grown-up daughter acting out compulsive sexual exhibitionism. Linda stresses that female sexual abuse impacts its victims with huge confusion: the mother who is supposed to care for her children mixes care with sexual acts. For Linda, the sexual abuse perpetrated by her client's mother was self-centred and concealed under protecting her children from seeing violence. Linda reflects on how it had affected her client deeply by her compulsive repetition of sexual exhibitionism, which was experienced as shocking to those who were present. Linda argues that female-to-female intergenerational abuse exists and that sometimes it is visible to us to see. I believe she is also emphasising that the trauma inflicted by the mother on her daughter had a powerful impact on her. The trauma matters and impacts everyone it touches.

Interestingly, during my training, a lecturer gave a similar example to Linda's, of a mother regularly sucking her baby boy's penis to make him sleep quickly. The lecturer critically commented on the possibility of seeing the mother sexually abusing her baby son. There was no opportunity to oppose the lecturer, and I felt silenced.

The Nakedness of Eve the Perpetrator: victimised, vulnerable, passive, and active

Helen:

> I saw a woman. The police broke into the property eventually and found her in bed with her daughter and her husband, all abusing the girl. It was the oldest girl, and it had been going on for years. The girl reported it to the police and, in the end, got out of the house. During the years of abuse, the father was so controlling, he wouldn't let her leave the house unless he knew where she was going. The problem was that the mother was incredibly unassertive, and she thought – there was nothing she could do, and so that's what she did: she abused her daughter. Her daughter was nearly eighteen when the police arrived, so it had been going on for years. At one stage, she asked her husband if something was going on, and he said no, and she believed him, whether she did...It's about cultural context: honour, family, shame, and what would she do financially.

A picture of a passive and trapped mother, not helped by society, is depicted. The mother joined the abuser, her husband, and became an abuser herself so as not to be the powerless onlooker anymore. Helen describes the cultural context in her client's family as linked with passivity, family honour, shame, and fear of financial losses. Therefore, the abuse had to be kept secret at any price. Exploring and comparing FCSA within different cultures and how specific cultural influences, belief systems, and ethnic backgrounds are linked with FCSA is beyond the scope of this book. Thus, any cultural examination focusing on Helen's experience with her client would be inappropriate. However, it could be said that in Helen's experience, her client's personal, cultural, and socio-economic settings seemed to make her feel even more powerless.

Helen shows deep understanding towards the victim/perpetrator female abuser, and it seems that within that therapeutic alliance, she holds those contradicting images in her mind: the mother as a victim and the mother as a sexual abuser.

Discussion

It is imperative to recognise that erotic transference is likely to exist within the therapeutic relationship. It is a process in which the client is oblivious to how the analyst has become the new libidinal object of the patient's sexual desires as a displacement from the original object. Usually, when a client experiences erotic transference and they are conscious of it, they are aware that it is unrealistic. Regarding another type of transference, a highly eroticised transference, sometimes experienced with 'borderline' clients, the 'as if' quality has disappeared, and the patient demands real sexual responses from her analyst (Sandler et al., 1992).

In circumstances where the client demonstrates and experiences an erotic transference or a highly eroticised transference, the therapist needs to be exceptionally aware of their countertransference when working with survivors and offenders of FCSA. The importance of awareness of transference and countertransference issues, arising specifically when a female therapist works with a female survivor of FCSA, is stressed to avoid any acting out the transference (Sgroi and Sargent, 1994).

The limited literature regarding erotic transference and countertransference within the context of working with F-to-FCSA sheds some light on this complex phenomenon. Transference issues are not avoidable when working with mother-daughter incest survivors. The therapist needs to be prepared that their client might interpret the therapeutic relationship as a re-enactment of past experiences of her mother's sexual advances (Ogilvie, 2004). Therapists can experience feelings towards their clients and act them out in numerous ways. The professional's and the patient's attachment histories interact with one another, and professionals must explore and process them and not deny their existence (Adshead, 2012). Adshead elucidates:

> Those who have had unboundaried relationships with previous care-givers may assume that lack of boundaries is the norm in any relationships where there are disparities of knowledge or experience. It may be hard to stick to a collegial relationship with a patient if they act 'as if' you are a seductive or cruel parent.
>
> (Adshead, 2012: 18)

Within the therapeutic relationship, and the pull to a re-enactment of sexualised parenting, it is the therapist's task to keep the boundaries and not act out sexualised transference and countertransference. It is stressed that the therapist must understand that her behaviour is the key to successful treatment. The therapist must deliberate on their own behaviour and how their client might understand that behaviour. The therapeutic alliance binds an effective treatment together (Ashfield et al., 2010). The responsibility of not falling into the trap of perverse transference lies with the therapists, and the clinicians must take every possible step to stop any risk of perverse acting out and crossing any therapeutic boundaries (Jones, 2012).

Any breaking of therapeutic boundaries, specifically not respecting the client's sexual boundaries, would be extremely damaging and abusive, and the most shocking boundary defilement. Any relationship between health workers, including mental health workers, and their patients cannot be erotic due to the power differences and lack of mutual knowledge (Adshead, 2012). Using erotic transference as a form of 'working through' (Freud, 1914) in therapy could be very frightening and hurtful, specifically to female survivors of FCSA, even if they are aware of the 'as if' quality of their transference feelings.

Still, whether there is an erotic transfer or not, the following therapeutic issues related to M/FCSA are often evident: the female client's fear of identifying with her female therapists, especially if she perceives her therapist to resemble her mother, possible ambivalent feelings about closeness to females in general, and her fear of becoming over-dependent on her female therapist (Ogilvie, 2004).

In the early days of my psychotherapy training, I met a female client who, during her first session, recounted to me her compulsive feelings of wanting to sexually abuse her female stepchildren in the same way that her mother had sexually abused her. After telling me about her urges, she looked at me with a long gaze and smile which went straight under my skin, while saying that she would always know someone who wanted to do similar things as she wanted. There was a nauseating erotic transference in the air projected on me. I felt an intense disgust and revulsion but managed to keep a blank face and expressed no reaction. The agency I worked for reported her to social services, and I did not see her again as she stopped her sessions. What has remained with me from this experience was the subsequent total lack of understanding by my trainee supervisor, who failed to acknowledge the seriousness of the situation and instead criticised me vehemently for reporting her, resulting in the prevention of her exploring her fantasies.

Themes such as the ultimate rejection by one's mother, the body being invaded by the perpetrator, self-harm, powerlessness, both the perpetrator's and the victim's psyche being invaded, shame, betrayal, the passive female perpetrator feeling trapped and the recovery being ongoing, are highlighted by all five participants. Ogilvie summarised in one sentence well that the mother-daughter incest survivors may:

feel such unbearable rage, shame, or fear that they may act self-abusively...Her strongly held belief that she is bad, that she is to blame for the abuse, that she is incompetent, unlovable, and disgusting activates feelings of rage, fear, grief, and anxiety.

(Ogilvie, 2004: 32)

The survivors feel powerless to seek help and reveal the truth about the abuse. Specifically, survivors of MCSA feel the necessity to keep the abuse secret to a greater degree than victims of other types of abuse (Ogilvie, 2004) whilst a female survivor of sex ring exploitation believes that she must be extremely evil from the depths of her being as she has forced people in charge to perform heinous acts (Herman, 2001).

The victim takes the blame and internalises the victim's and the perpetrator's all-encompassing shame as hers. Numerous female perpetrators have also experienced extensive traumas themselves and feel the perpetrator's and the victim's shame. In addition, many female perpetrators feel an immense volume of intolerable emotions of shame and guilt when their perpetrated offence is exposed (Ashfield et al., 2010). The overwhelming shame is so great that they focus entirely on their inner experienced evilness instead of considering their victim's pain (Mathews et al., 1994). The cycle of generational shame and blame is undeniable.

Summary

The impacts of FCSA can be visualised as a venomous six-armed octopus, swiftly altering its soft body into various forms and squeezing its way through the smallest holes. It is strangely split: its one arm does not know what the other arm does, and its several brains have distinct personalities. The mouth is in the centre, as if ready to consume all. Its ink is sprayed to camouflage, hide, poison, and cause blindness. Moreover, the octopus has an embedded propensity for self-destruction: its own ink can kill it, and the female octopus's death is caused by its cellular suicide (Nuwer, 2013). For me, the image of the octopus constitutes a powerful analogue of the impacts of FCSA. Both the survivor and the perpetrator are powerfully affected to the extent of the possibility of their psychic self-destruction.

Bibliography

Adshead, G. (2012) 'What the eye doesn't see: Relationships, boundaries and forensic mental health', in Aiyegbusu, A. and Kelly, G. (eds.) *Professional and Therapeutic Boundaries in Forensic Mental Health Practice*. London: Jessica Kingsley Publishers, pp. 13–32.

Ashfield, S., Brotherston, S., Eldridge, H. and Elliott, I. (2010) 'Working with female sexual offenders: Therapeutic process issues', in Gannon, A. and Cortoni, F. (eds.) *Female Sexual Offenders: Theory, Assessment and Treatment*. Chichester: Wiley-Blackwell, pp. 161–180.

Collins English Dictionary – Complete and Unabridged (2014) 12th Edition 2014 © HarperCollins Publishers. *The Free Dictionary by Farlex*. Available at: https://www.thefreedictionary.com/channel Accessed: 21 December 2024).

Freud, S. (1914) *Remembering, Repeating and Working-through: Further Recommendations on the Technique of the Psycho-Analysis* 11. In The Standard Edition of Complete Psychological Works of Sigmund Freud: Case History of Schreber, Papers on Technique and Other Works. Vol. 12 ([1958] 2001). Translated from the German by James Strachey. London: Vintage Books.

Herman, J. (2001) *Trauma and Recovery: From Domestic Abuse to Political Terror.* London: Pandora.

Jones, D. (2012) 'Therapy in perversity: Seduction, destruction and keeping balance', in Aiyegbusu, A. and Kelly, G. (eds.) *Professional and Therapeutic Boundaries in Forensic Mental Health Practice*. London: Jessica Kingsley Publisher, pp. 53–62.

Mathews, R., Matthews, J. and Speltz, K. (1994) *Female sexual Offenders: An Exploratory Study*. Orwell: Safer Society.

Nuwer, R. (2013) Ten curious facts about octopuses: Octopuses, octopuses, an inspiration for monsters throughout history, get a fresh look through a new book that dives deep into the creatures' mysterious lives. *Smithsonian Magazine*. Available at: https://www.smithsonianmag.com/science-nature/ten-wild-facts-about-octopuses-they-have-three-hearts-big-brains-and-blue-blood-7625828/ (Accessed: 15 May 2025).

Ogilvie, B. (2004) *Mother-Daughter Incest; A Guide for Helping Professionals*. London: The Haworth Maltreatment and Trauma Press.

Sandler, J., Dare, C. and Holder, A. (1992) *The Patient and The Analyst; The Basis of the Psychoanalytic Process*. Revised and expanded by Sandler, J. and Dreher, U. London: Karnac Books.

Sgroi, S and Sargent, N. (1994). *Impact and Treatment Issues for Victims of Childhood Sexual Abuse by Female Perpetrators*. In Elliott, M. (ed.) (1994). *Female Sexual Abuse of Children: The Ultimate Taboo*. Essex: Longman.

Chapter 9

Many faces, many levels

This chapter is divided into two categories, each consisting of multiple themes. The themes are listed below, but I do not dissect them further as I let the themes speak for themselves. The two categories are listed below:

1 Therapeutic work needs to be multi-layered and gender-oriented

   a Rigorous experience working with offenders is important
   b Challenging the present unfairness – gender-perspective approach needed
   c The importance of female-only specialised groups
   d Reparative, ongoing, and individual – working with complex attachments
   e The importance of community

2 Strong emotions evoked need to be processed

   a Impact of her work: strong emotions aroused
   b Processing her work crucial
   c The therapist powerfully and emotionally impacted
   d Connecting without fear with a trusted supervisor central
   e Recognising one's limitations vital
   f The therapist's self-care is fundamental
   g The therapist has limited experience; struggling with the octopus
   h The importance of using supervision and self-reflection

1   Therapeutic work needs to be multi-layered and gender-oriented

Rigorous experience working with offenders is important

Helen expresses an attitude of 'no-nonsense' towards sex offenders, ostensibly an attitude obtained from her long experience and multi-faceted understanding of complex work with FCSA. She states without hesitation that many psychometric tests are not normed on women and are not safe, while also acknowledging that some general tests can be useful. For her, listening to the women is a way forward

DOI: 10.4324/9781003607007-14

in therapy, as she prefers listening to what the women are feeling to measuring their feelings.

> ...some of the general ones, self-esteem ones you can use, emotional loneliness...but no, I don't normally do them, I just get them to tell me really how they're feeling, psychometrics haven't been normed against women cause there haven't been enough of them, so they're not safe enough to use really, they can give you a general idea and they use them at the women's unit but I don't think they're that useful or accurate even.

Helen asserts that it is important to work with female sex offenders individually and not to follow the therapeutic path as used for male offender groups.

In Helen's experience, her work with offenders has changed greatly since the early days of her work journey, as she states:

> I first started it was very much about an accusatorial sort of approach to them, about making them feel bad, and like good cop bad cop type thing...the idea was to break them down really and then build them up, and it didn't always work, because if you treat people like they are pigsty, they'll start acting like it.

Instead of treating the offenders as bad and 'pigs', and trying to break their resistance down, the focus is on listening and challenging constructively. The old, judgemental, blaming approach was problematic: if a therapist makes her client out to be a pig, she will start to act like one. I would add that if the therapist treats her client as if she were a pig, she assumes the position of a swineherd. In the therapeutic relationship, if you label your client, you also label yourself.

Helen:

> The whole approach has changed over the years quite dramatically, now it's about what they're saying, challenging them but in a constructive way, not accepting what they're saying, so you help them move from what we call the irresponsible chair of offending to the responsible chair of offending.

Helen uses a tangible object, a chair (metaphor), to communicate a message. The woman does not need to sit on the reckless chair; there are other chairs for her. This demonstration spells out clearly that the offender has a choice.

Challenging the present unfairness – gender-perspective approach needed

Sarah first calls on the professional to acknowledge the existence of FCSA. The second task is to adopt a gender-specific approach. She offers her personal experiences of navigating the difficulties of trying to assist professionals with accepting the complex nature of FCSA. Sarah has also developed intervention and assessment packages for female offenders.

Sarah: 'I have written several papers in more detail about the different aspects, the therapeutic aspects, the internet women…Because I believe women can change, I feel passionate about women in society generally. I am a feminist'. Sarah has extensive experience working with female sex offenders, and to be able to hear such an experienced person believing that female offenders can change is a source of hope.

Sarah's passionate voice articulates:

> I feel strongly that working with these women needs to be from a gender-responsive perspective, and it concerns me what professionals think – because those who work with male sexual abuse, they intrinsically know how to work with women. I believe very strongly that these are women who engage in sexual harm, not sex offenders who happen to be women. You need to be able to work with them as women, understand what being a woman in today's society means, what women's experiences are, and look at what gender and gender responsiveness means and integrate that into our approaches. I don't think that always happens, and although professionals are increasingly able to say: 'Yes, we know we shouldn't take what we know from men and extrapolate across to women', below the surface they still do, they just change their language slightly.

Although there is an increasing acceptance of the need for a gender-specific approach, Sarah is concerned that many therapists still believe they can work *intrinsically*, by having a natural ability with female sex offenders based on their working experience with male offenders. It is disturbing that some professionals who might not even know 'naturally' that FCSA exists seem to believe in having a natural capacity to work with this specific client group. In Sarah's opinion, therapists must listen to the experiences of female offenders and be able to integrate this core reservoir into their working approaches. Most importantly, female offenders need to be seen as women who sexually harm rather than sex offenders who happen to be women.

The importance of female-only specialised groups

Linda has established groups both for survivors and perpetrators of sexual abuse. In her experience, it is specifically within a group setting that trust and healthier relationships start to develop. This group setting facilitates a space where the dynamics between the mother and the siblings are repeated and worked through, and where the victims learn to confront their 'siblings'. Linda first learned about female survivors of FCSA through her work with a therapeutic group:

> I realised, when doing group psychotherapy, that women were talking about these problems in the group setting…this secrecy, the feeling of being favoured

and being abused keeps her away from any relationship with her siblings, therefore, they are not horizontal relationships. The abusive relationships are all completely vertical, and the group offers the possibility of horizontal relationships, but also to experience reality because they have to trust their peer group. And so, for the first time, they talk about that and sometimes they want to confront others 'their sisters and say, "yeah, mummy tried to do the same to me, but I told her off" so they will feel even more betrayed by this.'

In groups, the female survivors' shame is reduced, the power of secrecy is diminished, trust increases, and exploring the old, harmful relational patterns comes into view. The group functions as a family in which the group members can confront their 'siblings', the other group members, simultaneously working with their feelings of being betrayed by their original family. The transferences are horizontal rather than vertical, which creates tremendous possibilities for change. So, many of the old feelings and issues become activated and worked through 'here and now'. Although not expanded here, it seems that within a group dynamic, Linda functions as a mother/authority figure and, through her role, actively partakes in breaking the secrecy of FCSA. In Linda's experience, the group helps the survivors process their trauma on multi-faceted levels.

The importance of community

Mary's therapeutic mind-body-community approach originates from her own informative experience of recovery as being both a reparative and ongoing process. She avoids diagnosing and, instead, draws from aspects such as twinship and idolising one's parent. Mary believes that even 'untreatable' clients can find hope. Mary: 'I'm aware that it's extremely difficult for them to deal with one-to-one, being alone in a room with another female. No matter how strong positive transference is, there are still the wounds from their childhood'. For a female survivor of MCSA, working with a female therapist could be alarming, as she may experience the therapeutic space as dangerous. The positive transference could turn into negative transference by evoking fears in the victim of being seduced by her therapist. The childhood wounds are still alive in the therapy room; the survivor experiences these wounds in the present, not solely in association with a memory from the past. Concerning Mary and Ann, understanding transference needs to be comprehended in the specific context of both the client and the therapist being survivors of MCSA.

Reparative, ongoing, and individual – working with complex attachments

Mary:

> With someone like client Ann who had experienced abuse from when she was a baby, a lot of work is reparative, sometimes on Zoom she would often gaze

at me, you know, and it would be, I would hold her gaze and she'd say "it's really good to see you" and I would say "yes, it's really good to see you too." So, I think the mirroring is really important.

The reparative approach (by Kohut) is the backbone of Mary's work. Gazing, a central aspect of her approach, signifies a sense that one holds the client's gaze for a long time with wonder and admiration. The therapist connects with her own consciousness to hold her client in her mind, body, and spirit like a mother holds her baby. Gaze is a constant movement between two individuals that seems to have no limitation of 'real time'. Furthermore, in the context of a mother and child, the mother's gaze is internalised by her child. Gaze here is also without sexual desire; this is an important reparative aspect.

'It's really good to see you…yes, it is really good to see you'. Such simple words, and yet so transformative. Enjoying each other's presence and meeting again. Nobody had enjoyed Ann's presence when she was a child. To experience that her existence brought goodness to Mary was surely reparative for Ann, as voiced by Mary. In that mirroring, Ann could see her face in Mary's face, hear her voice in Mary's voice, and hopefully internalise her therapist's experience of wonder and happiness that she, Ann, exists. It is like a peaceful, reinforcing dance – forward and backwards in a peaceful repetition.

Using Zoom was very beneficial, and it seems that for Ann, it was easier to connect with Mary when there was a screen between them, as it acted as a shield to protect her from the possible dangers of intimacy. Mary is perhaps suggesting that therapists should work on a level that their clients can tolerate. However, I wonder whether a survivor with a history of being filmed by a paedophile group would have felt the same way regarding using Zoom, as it could act as a potential reminder of her traumatic past. Yet, that was not the case between Mary and Ann, who had established a therapeutic alliance and trust before having sessions online.

2   Strong emotions evoked need to be processed

Impact of her work: strong emotions aroused

Without a trace of hesitation, Helen talks about how her work impacts her life and her emotional landscape. She reflects on her experience of becoming vigilant, including her suspicion of the world inherently being a dangerous place, compelling her to protect family members who, in reality, do not require protection. She explains how she processes her work by carrying out practical tasks after each session and by connecting with her colleagues.

It is difficult for Helen to stop feeling alert even when there is no need for watchfulness:

> I don't like feeling that I should be so vigilant when I don't need to protect… it's difficult to explain. I mean, my close friend's sister got involved with a man who had a temper problem, they've broken up now, but she's got three young

children…I said to her if she had checked him out on the sex offender registrar, and she was horrified. She said that it was my mind that was impacted as they were labelling me as someone who was terribly suspicious. When my child was younger, I had all sorts of things in place, like passwords. Nobody used to pick him up from school without knowing the cat's name and things like this.

Helen's life has been significantly impacted by her work to the extent that she has developed automatic defensive behaviours, such as wanting to check that the people close to her are safe. Yet her behaviour brings distress to her family and friends. Helen laughed in response to her hyper-vigilance. I wonder whether her laughter expresses some embarrassment and sadness over the strong impact of her work on her personal life, including the time when her child was young. Working with sex offenders can dramatically alter the therapist's experience of life.

Processing her work crucial

Helen is forthcoming about her experience of becoming angry and frustrated when working with extremely perverted women, women who refuse to take responsibility for their conduct: 'If it's a difficult group and if the individual woman is very deviant or not accepting responsibility, you can get quite frustrated or angry…'. The word deviant comes from the Latin phrase 'de via': 'de' meaning 'off' and 'via' meaning 'way' (Harper, 2001–2024: no page). The female offenders have, in all respects, veered away from the 'normal' way of living; veered off the road of life without taking any responsibility for their actions, and that triggers anger in Helen. For her, not staying angry and processing her thoughts and feelings is vital: '…sort of just try and put it out of my mind because otherwise, I think in some sense they've got power over me'.

The therapist powerfully and emotionally impacted

During the sessions, intermittent episodes of implausible anger were felt by Sarah, which she would explore afterwards. She also felt sadness and, at times, would be so gravely affected that she would not be able to drive after the sessions. Processing her work was vital through proper supervision, as without it, she would end up taking her challenging work home and internalising it.

There were times when Sarah would feel her anger more acutely following the interviews (seeing the client):

I came out of the interview and just felt unbelievably angry, not knowing why, because there was nothing about the interview with the individual woman that should have triggered my anger to that extent. I needed to go away and process it and work out if it was something external to the interview that I had brought, that I'd been late, or had she been a bit resistant…was it something I had picked up from her and hadn't been conscious.

The anger felt 'unbelievable', meaning it was too difficult to believe. Furthermore, having no explanation for her anger, it felt like it appeared from nowhere. For Sarah, it is imperative to look firstly at her own reactions and behaviours and secondly at any external triggers. Before exploring any possible internal triggers, she reflects on whether her client might be unwillingly attending the sessions.

Connecting without fear with a trusted supervisor essential

For Sarah to have a supervisor's support immediately after an emotionally overloading session is crucial:

> I have someone I can phone and say I feel emotional when I need immediate good supervision at the point I come out of an interview, and just need you to talk about something inconsequential so that I can process what I've got and where I'm up to now. Sometimes it's not even safe to drive because I think if you've taken a lot of emotional, someone else's emotional turmoil, you need to be able to literally park that, as you can end up being not safe for anyone.

Being able to lean on the support from her supervisor by being able to talk with her supervisor immediately after the session, even about trivial things, allows Sarah to detach from her disturbed state of mind, relieving her from her client's emotional turmoil that she carries. *Turmoil* means 'a state or condition of extreme confusion, agitation, or commotion' (Mish, 1983: 1272). The impact of sharing a therapeutic space with an extremely confused and agitated client is so great that Sarah needs to let go of her emotions so as not to spread that agitation further and precipitate danger. This denotes in a significant way how the difficult material seeps through the therapist's skin.

Recognising one's limitations vital

Mary reflects on how, at times, she feels extremely affected by the sessions to the degree of questioning whether she is suitable for this kind of work. For Mary, having good supervision, both one-to-one and in a group, enabled her to normalise her feelings as well as become a clearer channel for her clients.

Recognising one's limitations is crucial, but it can be difficult to reach that realisation, as Mary conveys:

> Many survivors, we feel we can save the world and take on anything, but I had to be careful with myself. I did get ill at one stage, my blood pressure shot up, and I had to be hospitalised. That was quite an eye-opener, and as a result, I did reduce my client load and was able to refer on, which is always difficult as a therapist. I felt it was necessary. I do think it's important on a personal level to recognise your limitations.

For Mary, it took her body to collapse to learn that she could not save the world and that caring for herself was a fundamental prerequisite. The body first, mind later. I do relate to that: if one has survived sexual abuse by one's mother figure, it is easy to imagine having the capacity to survive anything.

The therapist's self-care is fundamental

Mary continues:

> To abuse that child pretty much from birth is absolutely heinous, it's disgusting. And I think that we need to, as therapists, recognise that and be able to have our strong feelings normalised because of that revulsion we start thinking, are we the right person to work with this client? Should we be working with a client who is going through all that? Group supervision is so helpful as it helps us to realise that this is entirely natural. This supervision space meant that I could be much more of a clearer channel. Hearing from other colleagues who were going through something similar with their clients and knowing historically that before I brought the drawings somebody else would have brought theirs from their clients...we all had shared experience because when you're working in that field you do need your supervision, you need group supervision, and you must have your own personal therapy.

Feeling such a strong repulsion for her client's issues made Mary question her suitability for working with this client group. These powerful emotions impeded her from thinking and processing her feelings. Yet, this process simultaneously taught her to be honest about her difficult feelings and prompted her to become a clearer channel for her clients. Channel means, for example, 'a broad strait, especially one that connects two seas'; 'a course or pathway through which information is transmitted'. Its embodied meaning in communication theory is: 'a gesture; action; sound; written or spoken word' (Collins English Dictionary, 2014: no page). The power of the shared experience provided embodied, emotional, and cognitive understanding that surpassed the utility of words. Additionally, the shared experience with her supervision group helped her to normalise her feelings and declutter her mind. Mary, utilising her self-care approach as a resource, was evident when her own trauma was re-triggered by her work; this prompted her to recognise the importance of having personal therapy, 'I did at one stage some years back have nightmares and flashbacks'.

The therapist has limited experience; struggling with the octopus

Greta's approach differs from the other participants. With an unflinching assurance, Greta describes how she is unequivocally honest with her clients. Empathy and reparative work are integral parts of her therapeutic process; however, there is no exploration of her weak points. For Greta, having both peer and personal supervision is central. She stresses the importance of being open with her supervisor and being able to process the content of her client's story, its impact, and her own responses.

Greta states:

> Well, empathy, compassion, and the reparative, I don't think I can separate any of those, in being 100% honest I don't think I do them – I think they are just part of who I am. I could no sooner take those out of me than become an axe murderer, I don't know how I do it or…I only know I do that because of the training I've done, I've always done it.

Greta said earlier, 'I think I'm a witch (laughing)'. Yet, in her experience, she is 100% honest and affirms that empathy, compassion, and applying a reparative approach are integral values embedded within her. Greta oscillates between extreme self-concepts: her epitomisation of trustworthiness and the impossibility of her being a murderer, while laughing when calling herself a witch. The metaphor of a witch carries a magical and manipulative connotation. Satanic abusers of her client used rituals, and witches are widely seen as part of ritualistic abuse. In my view, Greta seems to be struggling to make sense of her difficult therapeutic experience. There seems to be a huge split: Greta believes she is 100% honest, but there is no reflection on how she came to that conclusion. Is she avoiding taking ownership of her anger or criticism towards anyone, including herself? Does she wish to be the opposite of her client's abusers? After all, Greta said that some of her client's abusers were murderers and abused murdered babies. When analysing Greta's strong assertions of being 100% honest and embodying a flawless empathy, I try to contextualise it through her working experience: firstly, the client she worked with was undoubtedly very complex; this was a client who displayed several alters. Secondly, Greta did not have an extensive working experience behind her. She may likely have been overwhelmed by the complex work and significantly impacted by her client's internalised satanic perceptions, which were projected into Greta's self-concept through an image of being a witch. She explores projections and introjections in the next illustration. Nonetheless, I experienced Greta as a person who 'wears her heart on her sleeve', without any great filters, and this, I believe, is her strength when connecting with her clients.

The importance of using supervision and self-reflection

Greta continues:

> I talk about the content, especially some of the horrific content, talk about its impact or sometimes it seems to have no impact on the client, but then I think the more detached they feel to it, the more of an impact it has on me because I think there's a projection. They are giving me the feelings, projecting their feelings

through me, and that's often the toughest time when they seem to be fairly "oh yeah that happened, and this happened, it yeah wasn't great" and I'm sitting there thinking oh my god that's horrendous! So, I use both groups but mainly one-on-one supervision for that. I explore those feelings with my supervisor. I look at where my fears are; for instance, with one client, my fears of not going deep because I'm concerned about her safety. So, I am holding her back and too scared to go there, or is it genuinely her interests at heart?

Attending supervision is essential to process the sessions in real time, and Greta is aware of her clients projecting their feelings onto her. The more the clients are detached from their horrendous experiences, the more Greta feels and absorbs them. In her experience, her clients outsource some of their awful feelings to her to be able to feel through her. Perhaps the image of Greta being a witch emanates from a projection from her client onto her. Most importantly, supervision provides her with a vital space to explore the sessions in granularity and the ensuing emotions that they evoke.

I find the two previous extracts by Greta somewhat controversial as they partly contradict each other. According to the second quotation, Greta thoroughly explores her feelings as well as examines the emotions triggered by the work; meanwhile, the previous quotation paradoxically depicts a picture of Greta not fully exploring that which exists in her shadows. Consequently, I wonder whether there is, at times, an unrecognised parallel process occurring between Greta and her clients. This parallel process would likely entail an absolute detachment from all the badness, coupled with a suspension from all feeling. For me, her working experience provides a compelling and insightful picture of the struggles that a newly qualified therapist may face when working with survivors of F-to-FCSA.

Discussion

As stated by Helen, using psychometrics that are not normed against women is not conducive to overall FCSA therapeutic outcomes. Harris (2010) proposes the need for a gender-specific approach, including gender-exclusive descriptions, as women and men offer different perspectives even when they may appear to share similar pathological traits when offending. Several authors accentuate the importance of having a gender-responsive approach to female sex offenders that considers the role and influence of gender without labelling women or female perpetrators (Ashfield et al., 2010; Ford, 2006; Motz, 2008; Ogilvie, 2004; Welldon, 2004).

Linda emphasises the effectiveness of therapeutic groups for female survivors of FCSA. Such therapeutic groups nurture and offer support through non-abusive relations and exchanges (Elliott, 1994). Sgroi and Sargent (1994) maintain the positive effects of groups specifically formed to serve female survivors of FCSA by arguing that the group members demonstrate positive change as they start to engage with and exercise reciprocal dynamics of affirmation and challenge, as well as being challenged about their own cognitive distortions.

According to Helen, confrontational techniques, which have often been used for male offenders, specifically in the past, harm both female and male clients. Ford (2006) also questions the usefulness of argumentative techniques and wonders how impactful such methods are in responding to the sense of powerlessness many female offenders feel. The same has been confirmed by Ashfield et al. (2010), who state that individual women feel disregarded by confrontational techniques.

All five therapists have described intense emotional impacts when working with survivors and/or perpetrators of FCSA. Ogilvie (2004: 156) provides a comprehensive list of possible emotional effects on therapists who work with survivors of FCSA. These reactions could have culminated due to their own life experience or an incident that has taken place in the therapy:

> They may be easily shocked, irritated, or repulsed by the issue of mother-daughter incest. They may be dealing with the client's fear that the therapist will vomit on the spot and throw her out...They may feel intense anger...depressed or overwhelmed...highly emotional...overidentify with the client...overprotect her.

Welldon (2007) underscores that when working with forensic patients, a minimal requirement should be for the therapist to have personal therapy. Personal therapy enables the therapist to differentiate between what is hers and what is the patient's, as the narrative of a patient can be acutely distressing to the degree that a therapist can feel like they are working with material that can detonate at any given moment.

Summary

Helen, Mary, Linda, and Sarah emphasised and substantiated both the importance and need for gender-specific approaches when working with female sex offenders and survivors, whether in one-to-one or group settings. Further, the dissemination and availability of literature on FCSA are crucially needed by practitioners who might have never worked with this specific client group. Linda, an experienced group analyst, illustrated the power of groups, particularly from the vantage point of working with past siblings and parental dynamics. Mary accentuates how healing can be enhanced within and by a caring community, a valuable and reverberating reminder for us.

All the participants described the manifestation of their strong emotions as being evoked by their work. Linda's crying outside the session is described in the section *Bold empathy*. Helen reported becoming over-protective and extremely suspicious of people, while feeling frustrated and angry with the women who do not take responsibility for their offending. Sarah felt extremely angry at times for not having enough resilience to do the demanding work and occasionally would need to process her feelings with her supervisor immediately after sessions. Mary described feeling extremely sick at times after the sessions, to the extent of ending up in the hospital due to her work stress. Her emphasis was centred on normalising her feelings of disgust within the setting of supervision for her to become a clear channel for her client. Greta brought to the fore her need to process her clients' horrendous narratives and projections in supervision. While all the therapists spoke about the difficulties they faced within the complex work, what surfaced most palpably was an indelible hope for change that they all carried, for both the perpetrators and the victims of FCSA.

Bibliography

Ashfield, S., Brotherston, S., Eldridge, H. and Elliott, I. (2010) 'Working with female sexual offenders: Therapeutic process issues', in Gannon, A. and Cortoni, F. (eds.) *Female Sexual Offenders: Theory, Assessment and Treatment.* Chichester: Wiley-Blackwell, pp. 161–180.

Collins English Dictionary – Complete and Unabridged (2014) 12th Edition 2014 © HarperCollins Publishers. *The Free Dictionary by Farlex.* Available at: https://www.thefreedictionary.com/channel (Accessed: 21 December 2024).

Elliott, M. (1994) 'What survivors tell an – Overview'. In Elliott, M. (ed.) *Female Sexual Abuse of Children: The Ultimate Taboo.* Essex: Longman, pp. 5–13.

Ford, H. (2006) *Women Who Sexually Abuse Children.* Chichester: John Wiley& Sons, Ltd.

Sgroi, S and Sargent, N. (1994*). Impact and Treatment Issues for Victims of Childhood Sexual Abuse by Female Perpetrators.* In Elliott, M. (ed.) (1994). *Female Sexual Abuse of Children: The Ultimate Taboo.* Essex: Longman, pp.14-36

Harper, D. (2004–2024).*Online Etymology Dictionary.* Available: https://www.etymonline.com/search?q=deviant (Accessed: 21 December 2024).

Harris, D. (2010) 'Theories of female sexual offending', in Gannon, A. and Cortoni, F. (eds.) *Female Sex Offenders: Theory, Assessment and Treatment.* Chichester: Wiley-Blackwell, pp. 31–51.

Mish, F (ed.) (1983) *Webster's Ninth New Collegiate Dictionary.* Spring Field: Merriam-Webster Inc.

Motz, A. (2008) *The Psychology of Female Violence; Crimes against the Body.* 2nd ed. London: Routledge.

Ogilvie, B. (2004) *Mother-Daughter Incest; A Guide for Helping Professionals.* London: The Haworth Maltreatment and Trauma Press.

Welldon, E. ([1988] 2004) *Mother, Madonna and Whore: The Idealization and Denigration of Motherhood.* London: Karnac.

Welldon, E. (2007) 'Forensic psychotherapy the practical approach', in Welldon, E. and Van Velsen, F. (eds.) *A Practical Guide to Forensic Psychotherapy.* London: Jessica Kingsley Publishers, pp.13–19.

Section 3

Way forward

In this section, I present specific aspects of F-to-FCSA therapeutic work directed at survivors and/or perpetrators that I believe have the potential to assist therapists to work more effectively with these client groups. The following two chapters are presented:

Chapter 10 Bold empathy, a concept and framework that I have formulated and developed as an essential core component to be incorporated and applied to working with female child sexual perpetrators. This specific framing of empathy is directly informed and validated by the data gathered through the interviewed therapists.

Chapter 11 Conclusions and recommendations: guidance for clinicians, the last chapter of this book, presents specific guidance on the application of Bold Empathy for therapists, supervisors, and researchers working with F-to-FCSA. These recommendations are born out of the lived convergence between the analysed experiences of the brave therapists interviewed, and the childhood history and the therapeutic working experience of the author. They endeavour to introduce releasing pathways that are functional for therapists, as well as generating transformation in the lives of F-to-FCSA survivors and perpetrators.

DOI: 10.4324/9781003607007-15

Chapter 10

Bold empathy

Introduction

This chapter posits empathy as being both boundaried and bold. I wish to clarify that the term 'bold' must not be conflated with any martyr-style approach to F-to-FCSA therapeutic work. This specific conceptualisation of empathy directly evolved from the interviewed therapists who present a distinctive depth in their understanding and application of empathy. It comprises the prioritisation of the necessity of exercising extremely firm boundaries, whilst actively cultivating a deep empathy towards their clients. Bold Empathy, which forms the epicentre of this book, has been developed as an essential concept and framework when working with female child sexual perpetrators and victims. Understanding and embodying the function and application of Bold Empathy is equally relevant to therapeutic work with both perpetrators and survivors of F-to-FCSA. Empathy cannot exist nor fulfil its transformative capability without boundaries, and vice versa. The interviewed therapists working with female sex offenders had no illusions surrounding their clients' history of perpetrating or their capability of sexually abusing children. To be able to imagine, internalise, and express direct empathy towards these types of clients can be immensely challenging and ultimately requires courage. It demands a resolute willingness to not only engage with the complexity of the therapeutic material from the outset but also to remain unequivocally and empathetically present as the perpetrators' layers unfold, revealing their full human spectrum. Hence, I have called this type of empathy 'Bold Empathy'.

Bold Empathy comprises the parallel application of two core principles/mechanisms, each reinforcing the other: firm boundaries and embodied empathy. Firstly, firm boundaries are investigated; therapeutic work cannot exist without clear and firm boundaries. Secondly, the mechanism of empathy is delineated, presenting an empathy that includes and extends the parameters of thinking and feeling empathy, prioritising an empathy situated within the container and transmitter of embodiment. Embodied empathy is revealed as being integral to the fertile foundation of effective therapeutic work. Understanding the client's lived experiences is essential in helping the therapist develop empathy towards even the most difficult and seemingly 'heinous' clients.

DOI: 10.4324/9781003607007-16

In this chapter, the second movement of *teiro* – being rubbed away (Papadopoulos, 2002), as already partly explored in Chapter 9: Many faces, many levels – comes further alive. It contributes to a deeper understanding of the edifice of Bold Empathy.

The chapter is divided into four parts: (i) Importance of boundaries: the skeleton of the therapeutic work, (ii) Understanding develops empathy – therapist's use of self, (iii) Discussion, and (iv) A more detailed exploration of the notion of Bold Empathy.

Importance of boundaries: the skeleton of the therapeutic work

Linda, Mary, Helen, and Greta collectively depict mothers who treat their children as part-objects of their bodies. The lack of boundaries between the sexually harming mother and her daughter is well-researched (Glenn, 1984; Motz, 2008; Pines, 1993; Welldon, 2004). Gannon, Rose, and Cortoni (2010), on the lack of boundaries between the abusive mother and her daughter, suggest that the perpetrators themselves have felt out of control during their offending. This indicates that the lack of boundaries occurring on several levels is linked with the perpetrators' sexually harmful behaviour, therefore necessitating the indisputable urgency to ensure firm boundaries are upheld within the therapeutic setting. Sexually abusive mothers have violated boundaries; they have no sense of boundary recognition between the child and themselves, nor hold any boundaries that govern their behaviour, regulating their sense of feeling out of control. This demands the need to prevent re-enactment in therapy, hence the need for firm boundaries regarding countertransference, setting, time, and place.

The interviewed therapists demonstrate how they reinforce boundaries within the therapeutic setting. The importance of the therapist being direct and maintaining firm boundaries in the therapeutic setting is emphasised. Some of the measures taken to implement the necessary boundaries include: the use of appropriate clothing, the prohibition of verbal and/or physical violence, limited access to computers, as well as regulated visits of their children. Female offenders may at the outset respond with a refusal to accept any boundaries, yet after a period of processing, they accept that the boundaries make them feel a sense of safety. In other words, boundaries are an integral part of the care offered within the therapy (Ashfield et al., 2010).

Helen:

> I do feel quite empathetic towards them, but then, on the other hand, you have to separate that and their behaviour, which is illegal, criminal, and abusive, it has huge long-term impacts on victims, it must stop, and it can't be allowed to be repeated.

Helen voices the relevance of maintaining firm boundaries with her female sex-offending clients. Coupled with her empathetic working approach, she holds the unequivocal assertion that their behaviour is criminal and must stop. To stop the 'what', the clients' abusive behaviour, is non-negotiable. The sharp boundary that exists is unyielding. Some therapists may challenge this uncompromising stance, maintaining that it is not consistent with client-centred therapy. However, Helen is steadfast in her position: firstly, it is imperative that the abuse must stop, and secondly, the client needs to be cognisant of the costs and benefits of their abuse. This vicious cycle entails the woman first feeling better but subsequently feeling worse as the guilt and shame return, precipitating the need to repeat the offence. There is an overwhelming sense that for Helen, helping these women to refrain from abusing is caring for them deeply. Furthermore, providing them with alternative ways has the potential to instigate an exit from the entrapping vicious cycle of perversion.

Helen:

> We do go through costs and benefits with them: so, what have been the benefits of your offending – so they'll come up with sexual gratification (laughter and silence) that it felt good at the time. But then if you do the costs and benefits analysis with them, they can see that the costs were huge, you know they've lost lots of things, they've lost their families, self-respect, the internal things as well as publicity, maybe going to prison or going to court being and vilified as a female sex offender, being the lowest of the low, that's how they see.

The women are encouraged and aided to explore and face the costs and benefits of offending. The therapeutic setting may be the only existing space where the perpetrators can grieve their losses. When commenting on some women seeing sexual gratification as a benefit, Helen laughs. I wonder whether that laughter is an extension of an underlying displacement stemming from a dissonance in accepting the idea of an adult woman getting sexual pleasure out of a child.

Helen also reports that women are often vilified in courts. The word 'vilify' means to slander and defame. Her expression describes how communities despise female offenders and regard them as degenerate, as subhuman. For Helen, applying a multifocal lens to the experiences of female offenders, including their traumatic pasts, assists in developing a deeper understanding and empathy towards their clients. On the other hand, empathy can be regarded as a therapist's proficiency in trying to understand and relate to their client's emotions. Some women only know how to cope with their childhood trauma by denying it and thus resisting the treatment (Ashfield et al., 2010). Developing an empathetic understanding is key to engaging with the full picture and the multiple layers of the offender's feelings and behaviour. Labelling the female client does not engender empathy or understanding. On the contrary, it is precisely understanding and empathy as working in tandem that equip the therapist to work with these complex client groups.

Sarah:

> Sometimes we are not at the top of our game, and recognising that is important, I mean, I need to be very careful in an interview, maybe do a shorter interview

or park some difficult things for our next interview when I'll have a greater level of resilience to deal with it. Sometimes, I will close interviews: for example, if a woman is being hugely sexually abusive, by using very graphic sexualised language to try to emotionally bully, being aware that managing that in an interview is challenging and that I can only manage that effectively for a small period. So not allowing those kinds of interviews to go and for that abusive process to continue, – having the confidence to be able to say, we're not doing this – this is unacceptable. You will go away and think about it, and I will go away and think about it, and then we'll meet again. Some of that comes with age and experience.

In Sarah's experience, being self-aware both physically and emotionally is essential before going into a session. Sarah projects a mandate to stop the abuse in the session. The presence of an unbending deterrent is the antithesis of most ongoing child sexual abuse scenarios. Her message to the woman is clear: abuse is not acceptable, and it must stop. Sarah does not allow the perpetrator to use either abusive language or gestures during the sessions and will resort to stopping the sessions should that occur. Still, I wonder whether this draconian approach could result in the woman ultimately experiencing such closure as punitive. In practice, it can be interpreted as a version of, 'If you do not behave, you will not get the treatment'. However, closing the session seems to be an essential part of the treatment, as Sarah puts it, both of them go away and think about the session, then come back after some days and reflect on it. The difficult issues are not left without being reflected on and spoken about. Sarah's confidence to do such things, as closing a session, has increased over the years. I can imagine an inexperienced therapist not being able to exert the same level of authority and coming away feeling as though they are not a 'good enough' (Winnicott, 1991) therapist, while fearing being criticised by their supervisor for not having enough resilience.

Sarah:

> To desire to be the woman's friend and let's go through this together, is usually destructive for the client because she doesn't need a friend, she needs someone safe to tell things to. But I think there's a potential to get into that hugely disruptive dynamic.

Sarah warns about the nefarious impact of a therapist trying to become her client's friend. She asserts that the woman does not need a friend; she needs a safe therapist to talk to. Why would a therapist desire to be the woman's friend? Would the therapist pre-emptively use friendship as self-defence for the fear of being attacked emotionally or even physically by her client? This type of approach in the guise of a 'friendship' would destroy any therapeutic elements by blurring the boundaries.

Mary: 'That symbiotic relationship that survivors have with their mother makes it so difficult to have their own beliefs and needs and have their own opinions. To be separate from their mother gives them incredible anxiety'. For Mary, having a firm understanding of a survivor's relationship with her sexually abusive mother is key. The daughter does not seem to exist autonomously from her mother, nor able to function as a separate being. She has no chance to know her own mind, as her existence has been based on her mother's wishes and desires. Therefore, having firm boundaries is essential.

Mary:

> I think I can understand Ann in some ways. I had a series of therapists, and I found it very hard to keep a connection, understandably, and so I wouldn't turn up, or come late. In the end she said to me "This is not going to happen in the future, what I want you to do is to pay in advance," and I said "well I can't I'm a single parent," and she said "no what we'll do is, we'll do it in instalments, so each week you pay until you're in advance, and then anytime you don't come I keep the money. You know if you don't come, you're wasting your money, I'm wasting my time." I hated her, I give that example repeatedly to clients. If you don't come, you have to pay, and she saved my life ultimately because if she hadn't done that, then I don't believe that I would have been able to keep going, you know, because I was messing about and feeling depressed. I was very chaotic, and she gave me structure, and I had to keep to it, and it hurt me and my purse, so I thought well I have to go, and this is what clients do they laugh at me and say, "I don't want to come but because I have to pay, I have to come.

For Mary, learning to respect her own space and feel respected by her therapist was essential for the development of her sense of self. During her recovery, Mary's therapist established a contract of making regular payments to help her learn to value the therapeutic relationship and space. It was those first detested ground-laying boundaries that helped her to gain structure and navigate her depression and confusion. The boundaries acted as motivational prompts that kept her going to therapy. Mary made sense of her own experience of needing to have firm boundaries and established similar ones with her clients. She discusses later in her interview how, ultimately, it is the offender who should pay for therapy; yet, by paying, the client is doing something positive for herself, which can further motivate her to attend the session. The survivor of FCSA is likely to have ambivalent feelings about becoming attached to her therapist. When negotiating professional boundaries, it is crucial to comprehend that the attachment with the female therapist by a female survivor of CSA can be experienced as dread and peril. The therapist should bear in mind that there is no place in the therapeutic relationship to dominate the victim and victimise her further (Ogilvie, 2004).

Linda: 'Then you see, there are different situations, some women treat their children like a fetish'. Fetish means:

> an object of irrational reverence or obsessive devotion...an object or bodily part whose real or fantasised presence is psychologically necessary for sexual

gratification and that is an object of fixation to the extent that it may interfere with complete sexual expression.

(Mish, 1983: 458)

The child does not have her agency, and the mother regards her as part of her body, both emotionally and physically, by symbolically breaking the skin of separation given at birth between her child and herself.
Linda:

It is very important to detach yourself from the situation. When you feel emotional, you lose your sense of reality and your sense of thinking. You are not equipped to think. We must, at that point, suspend all emotion and then just look at this woman and see. It's extremely important to get yourself in a state of understanding.

From Linda's perspective, having boundaries is immensely important during the therapeutic session. The client's skin should not be pierced by the therapist's interventions, the therapeutic relationship, or the lack of them. In relation to the therapist's role in the initial stages of trauma work, Anzieu (1993 in Ingham, 2004: 101) poignantly illustrates the opposite of this breaching of the client's boundary:

the pain caused is less if someone can be found as quickly as possible to function, both by the words they speak and the attention they give, as an auxiliary or substitute skin ego (or envelope) for the injured person.

To protect herself from becoming emotionally entangled with her client, the therapist needs to suspend all her emotions. The detachment facilitates experiencing the client as she appears, without being clouded by emotional assumptions. Furthermore, becoming emotional hinders the therapist from thinking. The emotional and cognitive boundaried therapeutic space should not be traversed by the therapist's feelings. Someone might wonder how an emotionally detached therapist can help her client. The limitation of expression is applied for the benefit of the therapy. Linda demonstrates the importance of not expressing their emotions to the clients to facilitate a space where the client's voice and presence can be engaged with. Mary earlier on stresses the importance of being aware of her facial expressions and wanting to be like a blank screen.

Understanding develops empathy – therapist's use of self

Whilst Linda explores the need for the therapist to suspend her emotions in the previous section and is very boundaried with her client during the sessions, outside of the sessions, she cries for her, feeling her pain and emptiness under her skin.

Linda also experiences an internal conflict of protecting the baby while depriving the perpetrator-mother of having her baby. According to her, we always fall into the place where the client is. I believe that it is through that 'falling' that therapists can gain empathy towards their clients.

Linda asks whether we have the capability of recognising, seeing, and understanding these women, women who are simultaneously both survivors and offenders of FCSA. Or are we blinded by our feelings and assumptions? The therapist must manage their own emotions while working with their clients for the work to be beneficial. Suspending emotions and/or managing them goes hand in hand with understanding the client (Ashfield et al., 2010).

Linda mourned her client's loss, which aided her in gaining a deeper empathy for her client's barren life after her child was taken away. I believe that Linda's experience of working with extremely firm boundaries and embodied grief encapsulates what Bold Empathy can look like in action. The embodiment of the female victims/perpetrators' grief by the female therapist comprises an essential dimension of practising Bold Empathy. In most instances, the female perpetrators do not have the right or the possibility to mourn the loss of their removed/confiscated children. Yet, acknowledging the need for female offenders to receive empathy is critical to facilitate them to feel empathy towards others, including those they have hurt (Ashfield et al., 2010).

Linda:

> I had to write this report recommending she not be in charge of her baby, and I felt so bad that I said to myself, I want to get out of this situation. I went to an art exhibition to give myself a sort of different feeling, which at that point was at the Royal Academy, and when I was there, I went to a statue of a woman with two arms extended with nothing in her arms. I couldn't stop crying there because I saw exactly what this girl would face soon, so yes, in a way, this work does affect me, and it's silly to say that it doesn't. I realised the case has gone under my skin.

Linda voices how she was able to empathise with her client's maternal pain when her child was taken away, as a direct consequence of Linda's professional recommendation being involved with the case. This illustrates how Linda's professional responsibilities do not prevent her from empathising with her client's loss. Linda's personal shield had been broken, and the case had gone under her skin. Linda describes embodying her client's pain, to the extent that when faced with a statue of a woman stretching her arms out to emptiness, she could not stop crying. This extract illustrates the dual professional and personal conflict within Linda: she has the authority to both protect the child by separating the child from the mother, as well as letting her have the child and risking further abuse. Although Linda asserts that detaching from one's emotions is important during the sessions, her emotions surface subsequently. She recognises that she feels deeply about the case outside her work, to the degree of regarding it as 'silly' if someone claims not to be affected by such challenging work.

Linda:

> You always must remember that, in a way, we fall into exactly what the patient is going through. When John Major was our prime minister and those two boys tortured and eventually killed the other boy, what did he say the following day? He said, "It's time for us to understand less and to punish more," which was exactly an identification with the aggressor.

Linda compellingly ascertains at one point or another that we will inevitably fall into the same place our client occupies. She gives the example of John Major falling into the place of an aggressor by demanding that we punish more and understand less. By adopting Linda's vantage point, it can be understood that if at times, the therapist falls into the place of an aggressor and/or a victim, then being in that place, whilst exercising a process of reflection and awareness, will ultimately deepen the therapist's understanding of her client's experience as well as the specific dynamics within FCSA. The therapist can't operate from the exterior of those dynamics. The suspension of emotions includes the suspension of judgement, which enables an application of empathy and understanding towards the client's position. For Linda, detaching from one's emotions and falling into the place of one's client to gain a deeper understanding is vital.

Helen:

> I do feel sorry for the women because you get a full picture of their lives: how sad and emotionally bereft lives they have. I feel sorry that their lives have been such a mess and that they've chosen…they're trapped in a cycle of abuse, both their own and the behaviour that they're into. They have no other way of meeting their needs apart from abusing a child, which must be awful for them.

Understanding the deeply fractured pasts of her clients and the depth of their entrapment in the abusive cycle helps Helen to feel empathy towards the female sex offenders. The word trapped means being lured and ambushed. In Helen's experience, abusive women choose to stay trapped in the abusive cycle. What the women choose to disclose to Helen about their past and present, together with how Helen perceives their stories, produces a governing dynamic that impacts the therapeutic relationship. In other words, the therapeutic relationship, in Helen's experience, does not exist in isolation from the women's stories. Helen sees the many layers of the picture as well as recognising a vast barrenness, an empty landscape of robbed lives, which percolates into the sessions and the therapeutic relationship.

Helen:

> Sometimes I think about my sort of dark side, it sounds bizarre, we've all got it, but if I'd actually had a completely boundaryless life, and I had then met my own needs at the expense of other people, I can see how people get there. So, I

can see where she's coming from...I don't like that bit about myself, but when I worked in the crown court looking at the horrible murders – we had to read the depositions – and sometimes I was like fascinated and horrified at the same time.

In this passage, Helen reveals the therapeutic value in imagining and imbibing the client's position. The simulation exercise of envisaging herself as being a person without any boundaries, solely focused on meeting her needs at the cost of others, enables her to understand better sexually offending women whilst increasing her awareness of how fortunate she is for not feeling such attraction towards children. Her fascination with horror stories, at work and home, is part of her bizarre side. The term bizarre means: 'extravagant, or eccentric in style or mode,...involving sensational contrasts or incongruities' (Mish, 1983: 155). Positioning her own darker side as a resource may seem counterproductive; however, her work is dark and full of incongruities, and she finds that she needs to dive deep into her murky waters to feel empathy and gain understanding of the murky waters belonging to her clients.

The female therapist's ability to hold her complexity without needing to separate herself from it and project it onto the client constitutes a further essential component of Bold Empathy. This is seen in the case of Helen. Helen's experience of identifying the dark aspects within herself demonstrates how processing these internal ambiguities directly contributes to her work being effective. Helen explores her fascination with the dark and cruel stories, and how her upbringing socialised her not to act on taboos. It is through her reflections that she gains empathy towards the offenders. Therapists need to confront their sadistic feelings, not only as a form of countertransference but also to face their dark side and consider the possibility that, under extreme pressure, they might also be murderers (Herman, 2001).

Sarah's emotional call for professionals and society to wake up and hear what the forgotten victims and perpetrators of F-to-FCSA are telling them is invaluable. Sarah's powerful embodied voice comes through for me as a poem:

> Somebody needs to have an interest.
> In these women
> Yes, in these women.
> And jump up and down.
> And say!
> Don't forget about them,
> Yes, do not forget about them.

Sarah:

We need to have voices for the victims of these women, I feel very strongly that the victims of these women are overlooked and forgotten – they don't get service because people don't think women can abuse. And if they do try from a victim perspective sometimes, they get a response that isn't always helpful because the primal dynamics, particularly with maternal abuse, are not recognised, and the victims still need to talk about their mum…many victim organisations demonise the abuser, which for these victims isn't helpful. They need to be supported. What happened to them was abusive, but also…There were bits about mum which were very important.

Many therapists fail to understand the primal dynamics of MCSA, such as the victims' need to talk about their mothers, who often have been their primary attachments. Sarah claims that organisations helping victims frequently demonise the sexually abusing mother, which is not helpful. I agree with Sarah that for the victim to have a mother or maternal figure who has perpetrated sexual harm is extremely complicated. The victim can simultaneously feel hatred, love, and longing towards her sexually harming mother. It remains imperative that professionals need to listen carefully to what victims say, and not base their help on their assumptions.

Sarah:

Spending time to identify with them the non-verbal cues that they possibly haven't been hugely conscious of, we try to bring into consciousness that shared language, which isn't always verbal language, that we can try to understand exactly what's going on in the session. So, from then on in, I can say to them, I can see your foot is tapping something…You know something's going on here that isn't good for you. Can we try and work out finding that language to unpick some of that, to address some of the transference issues of what they're transferring across to me, and bring it into the room in a way that we can talk about? I find that doing work around emotional regulation and appending a language for that at the early stages of our contact together is probably one of the best ways to enable us to try and move away from that transference that I'm getting something, which I have to extrapolate back to them…It's a long, slow process.

Sarah underscores the value of creating a shared and unique language from the first session, which can foster deeper relationships and understanding. She asks the women to identify their feelings verbally, but often they struggle to do that. While Sarah does not expand on why her clients cannot identify their feelings, there is an underlying understanding that those women did not grow up with a mirroring attachment figure aiding them to identify their feelings, consequently developing an emotional language. Hence, they had to create another language, the embodied language.

Sarah perceives her client's body as expressing something and encourages her to express verbally what her body is communicating. Furthermore, she contends that many issues can be explored and brought into consciousness through a shared language, including what the client is transferring across to her. Understanding precisely what the client is saying verbally and non-verbally is crucial with perpetrators of FCSA. Pertaining to the transference, there is an understanding of a shared language whereby the client feels safe enough to transfer feelings and thoughts onto her therapist and into the tangible space of the room, whilst being provided the assurance that what they've kept hidden their entire lives will be acknowledged and contained. That shared language becomes a channel between the two. The intangible becomes tangible: the uninformed language/thoughts and unidentified emotions become verbalised thoughts and identified emotions. Sarah uses the expression of *'appending'* a language. *Appending* means 'to add as a supplement' (Mish, 1983: 96). The language developed by the therapist and the client is based on the existing language, yet contributing to it is a major addition in terms of the development of meaning. For Sarah and her client, working on emotional regulation, including both the management of strong reactions and emotions and the appendage of a shared language, seems to be a vital part of addressing the transference and having it projected back to the client. Although the development of a shared language is a complex and cumulative process, it is essential. Sarah says it all in her next poem-like declaration:

> We're both able to agree
> That's what you're telling me
> and I've got you agree
> This is what you're telling me
>   And I've heard this is
>   What you're telling me.

She explains how the development of shared language includes understanding the client's non-verbal signals, as well as understanding her own emotions and countertransference feelings, such as anger. Therapists are encouraged to establish therapeutic bonding with their clients by creating a shared language and understanding its specific meanings (Ashfield et al., 2010). Stern (2002) movingly describes how the relationship between the infant and the child appears early on like a dance, the mother playfully connecting verbally and bodily to her baby and waiting for her responses. The mother and baby: gazing, making noises, being silent, touching, and the baby eating while the mother is feeding. Sarah's and her clients' interactions shared a resemblance with this analogy.

Whilst exploring various conceptualisations of communication, it is relevant to examine some philosophical concepts relating to shared participation and language. Merleau-Ponty states that

> Probably the chief gain from phenomenology is to have united extreme subjectivism and extreme objectivism in its notion of the world or of rationality... To say that there exists rationality is to say that perspectives blend, perceptions confirm each other, a meaning emerges.
>
> (2012 [1962]: xix–xx)

Gadamer (2012: 291) builds on the understanding that communication is more like a participatory event facilitating the existence of past and present, as he describes,

'Understanding is to be thought of less as a subjective act than as participating in an event of tradition, a process of transmission in which past and present are constantly mediated'. Finlay (2011) brings an embodied understanding of language by exploring Gendlin's ideas and asserts that the body is language, and language is alive in the body. She establishes a 'responsive order' in which the body brings forward the true meaning of the language, bringing together the senses of the embodied worlds.

However, a challenge regarding the formation of this shared language relates to the allocation of the length of therapy. In other words, if the female client has not been offered long-term help, then there is limited scope for the fundamental task of establishing a shared language to evolve.

Mary:

> It was extremely hard, and I remember that I was pretty much silent for a lot of it. It was an outpouring. I also had to be aware of my facial expressions. Having worked with many survivors, one size won't fit all: it's working with the individual. With Ann, I had to be as blank a screen as I could, because she had to get it out.

Mary struggled with maintaining this 'blank screen' position, suspending all expression, and sitting mainly in silence, while perhaps Mary also experienced it as an outpouring of their silences and voices. The word 'screen' applied by Mary can signify both protection and a canvas for a motion picture. In this respect, the varying meanings of the word 'screen' can be applied to offer an understanding that speaks directly to the specific needs and objectives of both Ann and Mary. Ann could have her motion picture portraying herself displayed through the mirror image of Mary. Concurrently, Mary could also use her screen to protect and conceal her emotional expressions, to provide a therapeutic space that Ann can inhabit. The specificity of working with survivors is determined by its case-by-case nature; there is no single approach that fits everyone. Mary reflects on the chaotic nature of her life at the beginning of her recovery process.

Mary:

> And she, bless her, was so afraid that what she had been through would haunt me. She used to check with me 'Are you okay?' also because she knew I was a survivor. I had to reassure her and let her know about the supervision and the personal therapy I was having, and she was very concerned about my well-being…I remember afterward feeling physically sick from the things that I had heard and what she was going through. It can play with your mind because I am a survivor as well, it can be triggering. I have had extra therapy and cried a lot more about my personal experiences. With Ann, I was very maternal, but I had to be very aware of my parallel processing, and that my experiences didn't pollute the therapy with Ann.

Ann's awareness of Mary also being a survivor of MCSA played a definitive role in leading her to have therapy with Mary; she hoped this additional aspect would help her. This added value of relatability between them is emphasised by Mary, who expresses how their shared trauma experience impacted the therapeutic relationship. Her usage of the word 'haunt' connotes a sense of dark memories being conjured/a ghost from the past returning. It is not unusual for therapists to account for eerie, weird images and visions when working with survivors of CSA that may be felt as unreal experiences of dissociation (Herman, 2001).

At times, it seems as though Ann momentarily saw herself as Mary's protector insofar as fearing becoming the one causing hurt. Those fears had to be identified and processed with Mary in the therapeutic space. Mary's expression 'bless her' encapsulates empathy towards Ann for being concerned about her wellbeing. The shared experience and its impact on the therapeutic relationship are verbalised and evident, thus creating a powerful channel between them.

This powerful channel at times resulted in strong somatic reactions with Mary embodying her client's narratives as well as hers and Ann's traumas to such an extent that she would become physically sick. Furthermore, the embodiment of the shared channel is demonstrated through Mary adopting a maternal approach with Ann. Mary reflects on her maternal way of being with Ann and her understanding, asserting that her mothering approach would have been hugely different from Ann's mother's. Yet, I wonder whether Ann ever associated/identified Mary with her own abusive, hurting, and seducing mother. Whilst Mary did not explore this, she underscored the importance of not polluting the therapy with her own traumatic experiences. Mary, a survivor herself, felt an embodied empathy and pain that often entailed her feeling sick after the session with Ann. The parallel processes and mirroring are very tangible between Mary and Ann.

Greta's maternal approach deployed during the therapeutic sessions builds on Mary's recognition of the importance of maintaining boundaries within the mothering approach.

> I'm very maternal in that I work maternally, but I'm conscious of doing it and constructively use that part of me within a framework. I think that if I wasn't aware of that, and I would become very motherly because that is part of who I am, and not knowing oneself and working this way could become dangerous – it would become about you and not about what the client needs. So, I've always got that little voice inside me saying, "Okay, you can be the mother figure, but don't be the mother."

Being conscious of being a maternal therapist is a key requisite for how the therapeutic boundary is formed. Without the awareness, the maternal approach becomes harmful and operates as a way of fulfilling the therapist's unconscious needs. There is an 'as if' symbolic quality of maternal care, but not a symbolic equation. Issues of mothering are central in F-to-FCSA and similarly essential when working with it within the therapeutic relationship. How does the female survivor of FCSA experience her female therapist? Does she experience her as a controlling, suffocating, and rejecting female? Or does she experience her as the ideal mother she never had? The issues of being a female therapist to a female survivor of F/MCSA are complex. Greta emphasises that mothering must be done constructively within the boundaries of the framework: 'I believe reparative work is the key here to offer that positive role model of a mother that might have been'. It is within the reparative model that Greta sees herself as a representation of a mother to her client. Yet, as mothering comes to her instinctively, a degree of self-regulation must be applied, by reminding herself that being a representation of a mother figure should not extend its symbolic parameter, as it is not concrete. Greta practices being 'consciously maternal' with her client and stresses that not having awareness can be dangerous. The importance of being conscious of the complex transference and countertransference feelings between female therapists and female survivors of FCSA cannot be highlighted enough. As some survivors may seek to have a female 'mothering' therapist, as a preparatory measure, the therapists need to face their past difficulties about mothers and mothering, separation, and possible desire to overprotect, for the therapy to be reparatory (Ogilvie, 2004).

The reparative functional value of deploying a malleable approach within the therapeutic setting is brought to the fore and explored by Greta.

> Sometimes you think, "god, I can't believe I just said that or did that, I'm an idiot". But so far, the things I've done "wrong", I've gone back and explored with the client, and the few times it has happened, it has been fantastic. It's brought out: how they felt, where it took them back to, the triggers that I've caused, and we've been able to go back and repair so much. You could never do it deliberately, it wouldn't work obviously (laughs), but when it has happened, and you've gone back, and you've owned it and explored it with them, about what it meant for you and them, it's been a special time.

When Greta recognises that she has got things wrong, she accepts her mistake. She will go through a process of reflection, which can include self-blame, taking ownership of the mistake, and exploring it with her client. For her, these therapeutic sessions hold significant value: the collective exploration of how her 'mistake' impacted the client, what it triggered in her, and the importance of the therapist's admission of her mistakes. This specific therapeutic process is very beneficial for a survivor of F/MCSA, as it introduces a new, diverging pathway of experiencing relational dynamics with female carers, one in which grievances are acknowledged and contained, and conflicts are resolved. This would represent a transformative departure from the original female/mother abuser who very likely did not take responsibility for her actions nor admit to the abuse being wrong. Greta's acceptance of her 'mistakes' constitutes a vital reparative aspect of therapy.

Greta stresses being honest about her mistakes. Rogers (1951) talks widely about therapists needing to establish a relationship with their clients based on genuineness, openness, and respect. When situating this approach within the work of F-to-FCSA, due to the secrecy of sexual abuse, the relations established by the practitioners must be respectful, open, and authentic (Ashfield et al., 2010).

In this regard, I find Todres' (2007: 99) statement of embodied empathy substantial. He asserts that if the therapist acknowledges a phenomenological presence within the phenomena itself, the therapist automatically becomes a participant, porous to a spectrum of experiences emanating from it, including both the emotional and physical. As Todres asserts,

> If the therapist embodies a phenomenological presence to phenomena, he is not just a listening or non-participant observer. He allows himself to be affected…It includes bodily sensations, sharing of images, and emotional receptivity to the phenomena encountered.

General understanding of the concept of empathy

It is important to bear in mind that there are numerous ways of understanding and defining empathy depending on whether one takes the view, e.g., person-centred (Rogers, 1980) or self psychology (Kohut, 2009). For Rogers, the notion of empathic understanding is as follows:

> …the therapist senses accurately the feelings and personal meanings that the client is experiencing and communicates this acceptant understanding to the client. When functioning best, the therapist is so much inside the private world of the other that he or she can clarify not only the meanings of which the client is aware but even those just below the level of awareness.
> (in Kirschenbaum and Henderson, 2003: 136)

Bateman, Brown, and Peddler (2010) describe empathy as locating yourself by instinct in another person's life experiences and emotionally identifying with that person's difficult situation. This capability of relating by the therapist and regarding their patients and their view without any bias is crucial. This is probably not something therapists are born with. Yet, it can be regarded as a learned capacity that stems from childhood experiences shaped by attachment figures, which is further reinforced during psychotherapy training.

Baron-Cohen (2011) stresses that we need to let go of our single-minded focus of attention: that person is solely focusing on their own mind or feelings; instead, we need to espouse a mind that gives attention to other people's needs and comprehends their minds to attempt to understand them.

Whilst these definitions and descriptions of empathy partly describe Bold Empathy, they do not constitute a comprehensive understanding of it.

Bold empathy

To provide further insight into Bold Empathy, I have re-cited Linda's profound statement that the therapists 'fall…into exactly what the patient is going through'. Linda seems to say that the therapist understands and emotionally absorbs the client's experience as she is experiencing it. Her statement offers a profound representation of what Bold Empathy looks like in a therapeutic setting. However, how is this different from the general descriptions of the concept of empathy? What does the word 'bold' mean?

Webster's Ninth New Collegiate Dictionary (Mish, 1983: 165) defines it as 'fearless before danger,…showing or requiring a fearless daring spirit, […], standing out prominently'. Bold Empathy refers to empathy that has a sense of being audacious, brave, and daring. However, could one claim that feeling another person's emotions is bold? The boldness lies specifically in empathy when it extends to the perpetrator and not just the victim, and requires the therapists to tolerate the frightening feelings that are evoked during the process of working with very disturbed clients. In contrast to empathy, the boldness in Bold Empathy relates to the therapists' courage to face the difficult feelings evoked in the sessions as well as the darkness within themselves, which ends up surfacing through the work. This darkness may include feelings such as excitement, fascination, fear, or revulsion, which they, in turn, find difficult to tolerate and feel defensive about.

The therapists must recognise that the empathy displayed toward a victim requires a different aspect of Bold Empathy from the one that is directed toward the perpetrator. This distinction stems from the therapist experiencing their disturbing feelings differently depending on whether they are working with a victim or a perpetrator. When working with a victim of FCSA, the therapist experiences their disturbing feelings as partly originating from the perpetrator, not entirely from the victim's pain. It is the perpetrator who has injected the complexity and the malignant impact of the abuse into them. Irrespective of whether it is a victim or a perpetrator that is being seen, both experiences present challenges. In some cases, there is both the victim and the perpetrator existing within the same person.

Bold empathy: theoretical framework

The following viewpoints provided by Klein (1995) and Ashfield et al. (2010) offer a conducive theoretical foundation that has contributed to developing the concept of Bold Empathy. The therapists face numerous difficulties whilst working with very disturbed client groups, yet despite these difficulties, they emphasise the importance of not retaliating and/or retreating. They demonstrate the capacity of being genuinely empathetic whilst experiencing difficult feelings toward their clients. While the therapist needs to endure their challenging feelings, it is also required that the therapist understands their client. Understanding one's client extends beyond the insincere pretence of withholding one's disgust and feigning empathy (Klein, 1995), which is rapidly detected as artificial empathy by sex offenders (Ashfield et al., 2010), and also by the victims. Moreover, genuine acknowledgement and recognition within the therapeutic alliance can powerfully enable the client to move toward their process of integration (Klein, 1995).

Klein's (1995) understanding of Searle's (1979) version of therapeutic symbiosis provides Bold Empathy a view into the internal processes of a therapist who willingly receives the client's body's non-verbal cues, instinctively understands what is going on between the lines provided by the client's signals, and lets their unconscious reasonings, informed by their life experience, enter their consciousness (Klein, 1995).

Therapeutic symbiosis is, by no means, a boundaryless collusion with the client who is and must be recognised as a separate person. Establishing firm boundaries is imperative, particularly with a client whose boundaries have been pierced by the trauma of FCSA. Understanding the unconscious processes enables the therapist to tolerate their own unacceptable feelings, such as aggression, as the therapist becomes aware of them during the therapeutic process. Although it is imperative that the therapist retains their capacity to empathise, the therapist must guard themselves against colluding with the offending behaviour of the client. Remembering the client's underlying feelings of emptiness, depression, and unworthiness that are at the centre of this behaviour can act as a deterrent to colluding.

Working with F-to-FCSA inculcates an emotive landscape that evokes emotional responses such as specific feelings and images in the therapists' minds, including helplessness, fear, and feeling entrapped, all of which can be hard to bear. Furthermore, the clients may project onto the therapist images such as being humiliated, abused, and sexually excited. Through a process of projective identification, the patient attempts to manage their projected parts by manoeuvring the analyst, as the patient needs to experience the analyst holding those projected split-off parts. Moreover, the analyst experiences empathy towards the patient because of their own primitive object relations, which become activated by the patient's projections (Sandler et al., 1992).

Bold Empathy emphasises the importance of understanding the unconscious processes and how they impact the therapeutic relationship. Often, the re-enactment of sexually abusing children is an unconscious behaviour. This unconscious behaviour needs to come into the perpetrator's awareness through therapeutic work so that the offender can stop the repetition of a vicious and perverse cycle. The cycle starts with the offending woman first feeling good about being in control, followed by emotions of badness and worthlessness. When the sense of guilt returns, it causes her to repeat the cycle of perversion, which in turn reproduces the good feeling. Uncovering the client's unconscious processes is the antithesis of what Rogers said about empathy and unconscious feelings, '...sensing meaning of which he or she is scarcely aware, but not trying to uncover totally unconscious feelings, since this would be too threatening' (Rogers, 1995: 142).

Therapists are not encouraged to partake in self-disclosure when using the understanding of Bold Empathy, as it could be regarded as a harmful clinical practice with this client group, potentially creating further fertile ground for sexual and other powerful images. Viewing self-disclosure as harmful contrasts with Rogers' view of the importance of the therapist to self-disclose to make the therapeutic work more effective (in Kirschenbaum and Henderson, 2003).

Keeping firm boundaries not only impacts the client and the therapeutic relationship but also strongly impacts the therapist. Linda remembers a case in which she had to alert authorities to remove the child from her mother's care. She kept the firm boundaries, but not without feeling the mother's pain. The consequence of keeping boundaries gave her clear insight into her client's pain.

The development of the concept of Bold Empathy is based on the experience of therapists working with F-to-FCSA. Yet it is likely to be applicable to therapeutic work with various disturbed client groups. The working context with F-to-FCSA is challenging, and the therapists can feel as if they are thrown between *The Devil and The Deep Blue Sea* (Analysis of Ruth), and within that turmoil, it is hard for therapists to feel any empathy toward their clients who lack all personal boundaries. It is crucial to be aware that it is not just the victims but also the therapists who are impacted both psychologically and physically by the clients who have traversed sexual and physical boundaries (Ruszczynski, 2012). Within these disturbing therapeutic relationships, therapists may feel assaulted by their clients, and it is at those points in particular that Bold Empathy is essential.

Merleau-Ponty (2012) provides a philosophical insight into the clinical situation and how the existence of both the client and the therapist is embodied and intersubjective. He inquires into the significance of our embodied being in the world in his book *Phenomenology of Perception* (2012). For him, the body is 'a work of art' (p. 150), 'the fabric into which all objects are woven..., the general instrument of my "comprehension"' (p. 235), 'a provisional sketch of my total being' (p. 198). He asserts that 'the body expresses total existence, not because it is an external accompaniment to that existence, but because existence comes into its own in the body' (Merleau-Ponty, 2012: 166). He writes:

> my existence as subjectivity is merely one with my existence as a body and with the existence of in the world, and because the subject that I am, when taken concretely, is inseparable from this body and this world.
>
> (Merleau-Ponty, 2012: 408)

He is explicit, 'I am not in front of my body, I am in it, or rather I am it' (Merleau-Ponty, 2012: 150). In other words, the previous statement, when relating to the clinical context, seems to convey that both the therapist's body and the client's body exist in their totality and interact in the intersubjective space.

The therapist's empathy must be embodied; it is vital that the therapist uses her 'self' to understand and channel that empathy, and in fact, all the therapists I interviewed reported using their understanding of how the 'self' had been impacted by their disturbed clients, to be able to work more effectively with them. Working with FCSA offenders and/or their victims is challenging on myriad fronts. For any therapist, it can be a frightening and disturbing place, especially when the counter-transference emerges in visceral, bodily ways.

Summary

Bold Empathy expands on the notion of empathy and is an essential feature of effective therapeutic work and relationships. Its emphasis lies in the therapists' capacity, to tolerate, process, and embrace their disturbing feelings and bodily symptoms, evoked through their work with either offenders and/or victims of

F-to-FCSA, whilst taking in their clients' disturbing experiences and images and processing them through a parallel framework of practising understanding and acceptance both towards themselves and towards their clients. This process enables therapists to feel a particular type of empathy towards their difficult clients. Bold Empathy is the therapist's capacity to use herself courageously to understand her client and put herself in her client's shoes whilst tolerating her own dark side. Klein (1995) stresses that if therapists are afraid of their own violence, abhorrence, or any other unacceptable feelings, they will be unable to work on this level and will not have the capacity to adequately sense their clients' feelings.

Bold Empathy is resoundingly evident in the work of the interviewed therapists. Through their voices, they demonstrate how by working with and through themselves, either symbolically or even in real terms by crying, becoming ill, or feeling distressed, they can develop an infinitely deeper empathetic capacity and range through which they can connect with their client more effectively. I believe that it is within this channel of embodied understanding that empathy can start to grow within the client. This will ultimately require therapists to be immersed in the practice of Bold Empathy, to contain, understand, and manage their own emotions whilst reaching out to their clients' infertile and debased lives, falling into the place where the client is, all of which constitute the unique and transformative therapeutic value and function of Bold Empathy.

Bibliography

Ashfield, S., Brotherston, S., Eldridge, H. and Elliott, I. (2010) 'Working with female sexual offenders: Therapeutic process issues', in Gannon, A. and Cortoni, F. (eds.) *Female Sexual Offenders: Theory, Assessment and Treatment*. Chichester: Wiley-Blackwell, pp. 161–180.

Baron-Cohen, S. (2011) *Zero Degrees of Empathy: A New Theory of Human Cruelty and Kindness*. London: Penguin Books.

Bateman, A., Brown, D. and Pedder, J. (2010) *Introduction to Psychotherapy: An Outline of Psychodynamic Principles and Practice*. 4th ed. London and New York: Routledge.

Finlay, L. (2011) *Phenomenology for Therapists: Researching the Lived World*. Chichester: Wiley-Blackwell.

Gadamer, H.-G. (2012) *Truth and Method*. Trans revised Weinsheimer, J. and Marshall, G. 2nd revised ed. London: Continuum.

Gannon, A., Rose, M. and Cortoni, F. (2010) 'Developments in female sexual offending and considerations for future research and treatment', in Gannon, A. and Cortoni, F. (eds.) *Female Sexual Offenders: Theory, Assessment and Treatment*. Chichester: Wiley-Blackwell, pp. 181–198.

Glenn, J. (1984) Psychic trauma and masochism. *Journal of American Psychoanalytic Association*, 32(3), pp. 357–386.

Herman, J. (2001) *Trauma and Recovery: From Domestic Abuse to Political Terror*. London: Pandora.

Ingham, G. (2004) 'Mental work in a trauma patient', in Garland, C. (ed.) *Understanding Trauma: A Psychoanalytical Approach*. London: Karnac, pp. 96–107.

Kirschenbaum, H. and Henderson, V.L. (eds.) (2003). *The Carl Rogers Reader*. London: Constable.

Klein, J. (1995). *Doubts and Certainties in the Practice of Psychotherapy.* London: Karnac Books.

Kohut, H. ([1971] 2009) *The Analysis of the Self: A Systemic Approach to the Psychoanalytic Treatment of Narcissistic Personality Disorder.* Chicago, IL and London: The University of Chicago Press.

Merleau-Ponty, M. ([1962] 2012) *Phenomenology of Perception.* Trans. Smith, C. London: Routledge & Kegan Paul.

Mish, F. (ed.) (1983) *Webster's Ninth New Collegiate Dictionary*. Spring Field: Merriam-Webster, Inc.

Motz, A. (2008) *The Psychology of Female Violence; Crimes Against the Body.* 2nd ed. London: Routledge.

Ogilvie, B. (2004) *Mother-Daughter Incest; A Guide for Helping Professionals.* London: The Haworth Maltreatment and Trauma Press.

Papadopoulos, R. (2002) *Therapeutic Care for Refugees: No Place Like Home.* London: Karnac Books.

Pines, D. (1993) *A Woman's Unconscious Use of Her Body.* New Haven, CT: Yale University Press.

Rogers, C. (1951) *Client-Centred Therapy.* Boston, MA: Houghton-Mifflin.

Rogers, C. ([1980] 1995) *A Way of Being.* New York: Mariner Books.

Ruszczynski, S. (2012) Personality disorder: A diagnosis of disordered relating. *Couple and Family Psychoanalysis*, 2(2), pp. 133–148.

Sandler, J., Dare, C. and Holder, A. (1992) *The Patient and The Analyst; The Basis of the Psychoanalytic Process.* Revised and expanded by Sandler, J. and Dreher, U. London: Karnac Books.

Stern, D. (2002) *The first Relationship: Infant and Mother.* London: Harvard University Press.

Todres, L. (2007) *Embodied Enquiry: Phenomenological Touchstones for Research, Psychotherapy and Spirituality.* New York: Palgrave.

Welldon, E. ([1988] 2004) *Mother, Madonna and Whore: The Idealization and Denigration of Motherhood.* London: Karnac.

Winnicott, D.W. ([1971] 1991) *Playing and Reality.* London: Routledge.

Chapter 11

Conclusions and recommendations

Guidance for clinicians

Introduction

This chapter makes conclusions and recommendations that are intended to serve as guidance for clinicians. It is written and guided by the innate intention and goal of contributing to the overall effectiveness of F-to-FCSA clinical work through the framework of Bold Empathy. It endeavours to introduce and generate pathways that are applicable and accessible to therapists, as well as engender meaningful and transformative change in the lives of their clients through the therapeutic work. All the themes are predicated on the analysed experiences of the therapists interviewed. The themes are clearly stated and easy to follow; however, they are not meant to be didactic, i.e., 'do this, do that', but rather provide an accompanying and informative resource that will ultimately better arm the clinician. It is my hope that the evolved recommendations that I put forward, born out of the multifocal, lived convergence between the analysed experiences of the brave therapists interviewed, and the childhood history and therapeutic working experience of the author, can offer an enriching repository and facilitate enhanced and fortified clinical work with client groups impacted by F-to-FCSA.

The chapter is divided into the following three sections:

1 Guidance for Psychotherapy:

- Awareness of the denial
- Reading available literature and having good teamwork
- Remembering and understanding the client's past
- Awareness of the impacts on the therapeutic relationship when working with perpetrators
- Developing therapeutic alliance with survivors and perpetrators
- Recognising the effects of working with offenders on therapists' private lives
- Suspending judgement
- Working with risk and safety
- Working with transference, countertransference, and projective identification crucial
- Application of multiple and gender perspectives modalities

DOI: 10.4324/9781003607007-17

- Understanding the heart of the work with FCSA – the Bold Empathy
- Accept your limitations and self-care

2 Guidance for supervision

- Supervision is an important space for the therapist
- Honest relationships between the supervisor and the supervisee
- The supervisor needs to be knowledgeable about the issues of FCSA

3 Advice for future research

Guidance for psychotherapy

Awareness of the denial

i **Awareness of societal denial.** The need to recognise society's denial of FCSA is vital. This awareness forms a fundamental aspect of being able to work with F-to-FCSA. Clinicians need to be aware of the nefarious impact that this denial has on the provision of gender-specific services for both the offenders and victims. Therapists colluding with society's denial of FCSA/F-to-FCSA hinders the development of therapeutic services and training.

ii **Awareness of the clinicians' own assumptions.** Clinicians must address their own assumptions regarding their perception of FCSA as being synonymous with sexual abuse and its related impact on the provision and effectiveness of psychotherapy. Clinicians need to be more aware of their own battling defences, which include being aware of their struggle to accept FCSA as damaging as well as their erroneous perception that deems it inconceivable for women to sexually abuse and even rape children. Therapists need to explore their feelings surrounding mothering and being mothered, specifically when working with MCSA. Clinicians can and should assume that they will meet clients who have suffered from the trauma of FCSA and F-to-FCSA so that they can be more accommodating when they encounter such cases. It is vital to understand that these client groups who have experienced trauma of F-to-FCSA display an inbuilt sensitivity that can detect a clinician's self-doubts concerning how they deal with work on this specific trauma. The implementation of this awareness on the part of the clinician is instrumental to therapeutic outcomes. If the client senses such uncertainties in their therapist, they will most likely refrain from disclosing their hidden trauma.

iii **Awareness of the sex offenders' denial.** Clinicians need to work with the female sex offenders' denial of their perpetrated sexual offence. The recognition of the denial will equip the clinicians to work towards the offender taking responsibility, as overcoming the denial is generally a major part of the therapeutic aim, substantially impacting the therapeutic work. The offending woman, who refuses to take responsibility for her perpetrated abuse, regularly projects her abusive part-objects onto others, including the therapist. Therapists must be conscious of the extremely challenging dynamic of the client's denial, as the perpetrator's denial and projections of their abusive behaviour often lead to an impasse which may feel intractable.

Developing awareness of the myriad ways that the female sex offender might deny her experience of childhood abuse trauma is crucial. For instance, the offending woman might talk about their experienced trauma, but then alter it into a different experience, even denying its existence, as the pain of that experience might feel impossible to bear. Additionally, the therapist must familiarise themselves with the potentiality of the offending woman being able to deny their present abusive behaviour, modifying it into various activities such as writing stories/drawing pictures for the staff members' children, or behaviours such as regressing into childlike behaviour.

iv **Awareness of the survivors' denial.** It is imperative for clinicians to demonstrate both cognitive, emotional, and embodied knowledge of the distress suffered by survivors of F-to-FCSA and to possess an understanding of the multifold impact it can have on the therapeutic relationship and clinical work. This understanding must encompass the extremely difficult reality faced by survivors, who struggle to accept that the sexual abuse was perpetrated by a female who was their mother/female carer, teacher, nanny, or any other female figure. The survivors themselves often feel that the abuse inflicted on them was out of the ordinary, leading to confusion and feelings of intense shame, and rendering it immensely challenging and distressing for them to acknowledge that what was done to them was sexual abuse and not, e.g., mothering, caring, and a special relationship. The clinician must accept that the survivor might find it extremely hard to recognise the infliction of the abuse on their lives. The survivor might feel that acknowledging the difficult effects of the trauma could equate to introjecting the abusers' characteristics into themselves, to the extent that merely imagining this possibility would feel intolerable. The clinicians may also need to recognise the complex issues related to mothering and being mothered, including accommodating space for the survivors to speak about the positive aspects of the offenders, if there were any. Talking about these complex areas can make the survivor feel exceedingly vulnerable; therefore, the clinician needs to tread carefully and embrace the client/the therapeutic relationship with bold empathy.

Moreover, clinicians need to work sensitively with the survivor's unconscious splitting between 'good' and 'bad' self-parts. This splitting is likely to become visible in the clinical setting as the survivor tends to be unable to face conflicting issues within the therapeutic relationship. The survivor might also divide the therapist into an idealised mother figure and/or a debased, abusive mother. Therefore, the clinician must work with a deep understanding of transference, countertransference, and projective identification. The therapist needs to work with these issues for as long as it is necessary. No survivor should be made to explore their shadow sides before they are ready to take that on.

Reading available literature and having good teamwork

Despite progress being made with the production of knowledge on F-to-FCSA, the overall inadequacy of literature on F-to-FCSA, coupled with the limited availability of training, especially for therapists practising in private settings, collectively renders a challenging and estranging F-to-FCSA working landscape.

Concerning scenarios where the provision of therapeutic services involves teams, the clinician must be aware of the divisions within the team regarding differing views and approaches to client work, to ensure that the team works in unison to avoid splitting. Preventative steps would involve exploring and understanding the differences constructively and working with the client, based on the integrated understanding. The implementation of a team approach is crucial when working with difficult clients within an institutional setting and is likely to strengthen the effectiveness of F-to-FCSA therapeutic work. The clinician must understand the importance of having an experienced supervisor from the initial stages of work. Furthermore, clinicians must understand that without adequate F-to-FCSA training, knowledge, and informed supervision, they cannot automatically assume that by virtue of being accredited therapists, they are sufficiently equipped to work with offenders and survivors of F-to-FCSA.

Remembering and understanding the client's past

The therapist must attempt to understand the client's past, regardless of whether they are a survivor or a perpetrator. The importance of hearing, understanding, and remembering the traumatic pasts of both survivors and perpetrators contributes to the therapist's deeper understanding and appreciation of bold empathy. Listening and validating the client's narrative, specifically the emotional side, is key to fostering a therapeutic relationship that the client feels they can rely on.

When working with perpetrators of F-to-FCSA, establishing an understanding of their past helps therapists to develop greater awareness of the causal factors resulting in the offender's resort to sexually abusing children. By cultivating this insight into their client's complex past relational dynamics, the clinicians also gain access to a deeper comprehension of the present enactments of their client's behaviour. Remembering the client's past offers the clinicians a more holistic perspective, which is not solely fixated on the abusive woman's behavioural and cognitive dysfunctions. The therapist should be encouraged to recognise that establishing an understanding of the client's past will fortify the therapist through the challenging times, particularly when change seems impossible and there is a deadlock in the therapeutic process.

For a therapist to evade the client's traumatic relational past would constitute a professional negligence of their client's pressing need to reveal their wound and process it in the therapeutic setting. To abandon therapeutic work on such a complex past and not recognising how it has impacted the client's personality and identity development, including the client's present life, can comprise a betrayal of the therapeutic alliance initially offered. Sessions dealing with survivors' and offenders' memories and exploration of past traumas and family contexts can be challenging and traumatising to the therapist. However, the therapist must provide therapeutic space for the clients where their experiences are heard and their narratives are validated. The therapeutic space should become a channel and a safe space for the survivor, as well as for the offender, to be able to grieve their pasts and losses, including their complex familial contexts. The therapist must be able to absorb and contain the survivor's and offender's pain. Many survivors of F-to-FCSA must learn to live with the fact that their perpetrators never take any responsibility for the sexual abuse they have inflicted on their victims. This reality should compel the therapist to inhabit the client's unresolved pain and the unknown terrain that the client is navigating, to help them process this difficult dilemma.

For the survivors, exploring the contexts of their lives can be acutely painful, as the experience of sexual abuse can be enormously traumatising and might require a considerable amount of courage from the survivor. It is vital that the therapist offers therapeutic wisdom and can hold space for their client, face to face, fortified by boundaries and empathy. The therapist may need to contain multiple processes that the client is going through, for instance, the client may be burdened by the perpetrator's shame, blaming herself for the abuse, carrying her family's denial of what happened, or questioning why nobody stopped the abuse.

Awareness of the impacts on the therapeutic relationship when working with perpetrators

Clinicians need to develop an awareness of how working with highly double-faced and split female clients impacts the presentation of transference, countertransference, and the clinicians' responses. This splitting within the client can feel overwhelming and confusing. At times, therapists feel disconnected and stuck. To develop therapeutic bonding with a childlike client who also attacks herself and others is complicated. Consequently, the therapist faces a quandary: will one connect with the naïve and innocent person who is like a child, or the adult woman who sexually abuses children? Therapists must recognise that, to navigate these types of therapeutic challenges, they will need to rely heavily on team support and supervision, which can be a lifeline.

The therapist must comprehend that understanding and consciously processing splitting behaviour within herself, the therapeutic relationship, the team, and the client is vitally important. The therapist needs to reflect on the splitting within herself as the therapist, as her position is exceptionally problematic: The splits between the private and the professional identity; between cognitively understanding her client while emotionally struggling to connect, feeling at times deep empathy while also feeling palpable anger for what the perpetrator has done. This process of identification of the division between the therapist's emotions and thoughts while working with the FCSA perpetrators is fundamental. If the therapist is skilful and aware of the splitting, it will enable the therapist to adequately process without becoming emotionally overwhelmed. Understanding the meaning and function of splitting plays a central role when working with these client groups.

The therapist needs to hold space for a range of extreme emotions and behaviour emanating from the client, including vulnerability, power, powerlessness, attacking, and the perception of being attacked. This is necessary for progress to be achieved. The therapist must be aware that the client may, at times, regard them as the perpetrator and consequently commit a physical or a psychic assault on them, as well as on everyone else within their relational context, including themselves.

Developing therapeutic alliance with survivors and perpetrators

The therapist needs to become a channel: a pathway that collectively connects the therapist and the client within an inter-subjective embodied space, enabling the client to express her feelings and thoughts. The therapist needs to understand the essential role of using herself through her emotions, embodied senses/feelings, and thoughts, to be able to grasp her client. For the therapist to become an embodied, sustainable channel, fostering an intimate and honest space and resilience, the therapist must engage in regular supervision and personal therapy. A profound key therapeutic wisdom can be movingly articulated as: The therapist always ends up in the place where her client is. This illustrates how a deep understanding of her client's world is gained. Understandably, this is not a straightforward nor an easy task.

It is pivotal that the clinician listens to her client and is committed to seeing her. The therapist needs to understand the efforts her client is making through verbal communication or their body language. The clinician must work towards creating a shared embodied language with her client: This includes the therapist developing an awareness of and studying the client's body language, i.e., foot tapping, eyes lowered, changes to skin colour and appearance. The client's embodied language often communicates feelings and thoughts that the client is unable to verbalise.

The therapist must be clear and consistent about what they want to transmit to their client, as both the survivors and the perpetrators of F-to-FCSA often come from childhood backgrounds where they would have received mixed and contradicting messages. Whilst verbal and embodied communications must be accurate and sincere, being blank-faced is also regarded as a significant way of being with the client, as it prompts the client to express themselves by filling the space with their own emotions, and not solely mirroring responses from the therapist's facial responses.

Recognising the effects of working with offenders on therapists' private lives

Therapists working with F-to-FCSA need to be aware of the varying and far-reaching impacts that their work can have on their lives. It can directly affect the clinician's sense of safety in her everyday life, resulting in her becoming extra vigilant. Issues such as therapists' pregnancy and having/not having children bear a powerful impact on the therapeutic relationship, as many therapists often feel that they need to not only protect their existing offspring but also their imagined offspring from psychic or real-life attacks. The myriad impacts of working with female sexual perpetrators are evident and can be felt on multiple levels.

Suspending judgement

Therapists should recognise that the equality between them and offenders surpasses the general debate of the therapeutic power relationship, as this type of equality can be located at a deeper level where the perpetrator and the therapist can meet within the shared inter-subjective space.

Every therapist working with F-to-FCSA should acknowledge that succumbing to judgement will only impede a therapist from fulfilling their therapeutic role and objectives. There is no place for judgement, as judging will ultimately hinder any connection with one's client by creating a pervasive moral hierarchy that places the one who judges above the one who is judged. Without a necessary structure of equality, survivors and offenders will struggle to connect with their therapist, and the therapeutic relationship will become synonymous with being a battlefield of power hostilities, camouflaged by transference, countertransference, and projective identifications. Even when it may seem impossible, it is imperative that the therapist and the client are positioned on an equal footing, and it is the therapist's responsibility to ensure that this equality transpires. This equal positioning acts as a vital deterrent against sadomasochistic dynamics from playing out. Equality in the therapeutic relationship is particularly critical when working with clients whose childhood has often been contaminated by harmful and threatening relational dynamics. Difficult therapeutic dynamics require self-awareness from the therapist, who must be prepared to reckon with any coercive enticements to give into reassuring and patronising responses, specifically if the therapist senses resistance in her client to work with her therapeutically. This resistance can emanate from both survivors and offenders of F-to-FCSA who have a strong propensity to detect any sense of inequality and power struggle within the therapeutic relationship.

Working with risk and safety

Working with the probability of re-enactments of the offender's behaviour requires therapists' expertise and insight. The therapeutic work may feel like walking on ice, which can fragment abruptly. Therefore, the therapist must be aware that re-offending is always a possibility and trusting an offender's words and promises is not sustainable. It is fundamental to encourage sexually offending women to become more self-aware of their daily behaviour, occupations, attitudes, and feelings by providing them with homework and encouraging them to keep a diary of daily events. The perpetrators need to be encouraged to plan and to have achievable goals, as accomplishing their goals will inspire in them a proliferation of resilience and self-awareness.

Working with transference, countertransference, and projective identification crucial

Understanding and working with transference, countertransference, and projective identification is key to avoiding acting out of transference or countertransference. The therapist will, at times, be viewed by their client as the abuser, which will parallel the therapist's countertransference. The therapists must develop awareness of the powerful dynamics of projective identifications of the perpetration and seek support to process these intra-psychic dynamics and how they impact the entirety of the work.

Specific attention needs to be drawn to erotic transference, as transference issues are not preventable when working with female/mother sex offenders and female/daughter incest survivors. The therapist needs to be prepared that their client might regard the therapeutic relationship as a repetition of their prior childhood experiences of their mother or their female carer's sexual advances. The therapist must acknowledge that the professional's and the patient's attachment styles and experiences act together, and clinicians must untangle, examine, and face their attachment styles and feelings. Denying their existence would endanger both herself and her client, potentially leading them to fall into a trap of perverse transference where the therapist can also experience varying emotions towards their client and be tempted to act them out. If the client seems to signal an erotic transference or a highly eroticised transference, the clinician needs to be extremely aware of their countertransference. The therapist must keep firm boundaries to stop and manage any pull towards sexualised re-enactments of perverse mothering and grasp that the behaviour of a therapist is the key and the foundation to effective therapy; it is the therapist's ultimate responsibility to consider their own behaviour and to explore how their client might comprehend their interventions and behaviour. Any breaking of boundaries, and specifically breaking a client's sexual boundaries, would be extremely damaging.

Important key points to recognise: The positive transference could turn into negative transference by evoking fears in the survivor and the offender/victim of being seduced by her therapist, as the repetition of childhood attachments is still present in the therapeutic relationship. However, the transference relationships must not be perceived as an obstacle to therapy, but rather as an instrument to help recognise the patient's inner space and how to connect with it. If both the therapist and her client are survivors of F-to-FCSA, the transference needs to be understood within that context. This requires a thorough self-reflection and awareness on the part of the therapist.

The importance of grasping the roles that are being projected onto the clinicians by their clients is critical. The clinician must deconstruct these projections into manageable comprehensions before communicating them back to the clients. It is through this process that the patient can learn more about themselves, and through it, this learning can develop into trust, thus strengthening deeper bonding. Without understanding and processing the projections and the projective identifications, the re-enactment of trauma will only keep perpetuating.

Application of multiple and gender perspectives modalities

Clinicians are encouraged to use at least two or more approaches, including modalities such as cognitive therapy, schema therapy, psychodynamic and psychoanalytic modalities, group therapy, self-psychology, body therapy, and art therapy, evidencing that not one therapeutic modality on its own is enough. Therapists also need to understand society's constructions around health care, the police, courts, prisons, and probation services, and how, e.g., misogyny and oppression of women have contributed to maintaining the cycle of F-to-FCSA.

The importance of therapists to develop a solid understanding of gender perspectives and gender-responsive modalities cannot be emphasised enough. Clinicians need to understand that when working with female survivors and female perpetrators, they are not solely working with perpetrators and survivors who happen to be women. Applying a specific recognition of the female gender of the survivors and perpetrators is of immense importance. Working with male child sexual perpetrators and male survivors of CSA or even FCSA does not arm the clinicians to be able to work with females impacted by FCSA as a benefit of their existing work experience.

It would also be beneficial to have a community/peer support system, specifically when working with survivors of FCSA. However, establishing and finding such communities as well as in-person therapy groups for the survivors of F-to-FCSA is not straightforward due to FCSA not being a common/widely reported phenomenon, and the scarcity of survivors seeking or finding suitable therapeutic help. The general therapeutic groups available to female survivors of CSA can be helpful, although the survivors of F-to-FCSA might feel that their traumas are not fully understood by the facilitator or the other group members. That is why it is essential that anyone working with CSA survivors also forearms themselves by developing a solid understanding of FCSA.

Understanding the heart of the work with FCSA – the Bold Empathy

Therapists need to embody Bold Empathy and engage with it as comprising the very heart of working with survivors and offenders of F-to-FCSA. There must be an imbided understanding of the absolute importance of keeping firm and unmovable boundaries, and that it is within those secured boundaries that empathy develops. Empathy without firm boundaries is risky, as it can lead to re-enactments when working with either FCSA perpetrators and/or the survivors of FCSA. The notion of Bold Empathy implies a therapist's multifocal capacity: maintaining firm therapeutic boundaries whilst practising embodied listening, and allowing themself to imagine, feel, and process the distressing experiences of their clients while also facing their own emotions and thoughts impacted by the complex work. Bold Empathy is the therapist's capability, whilst simultaneously bearing her own dark side, to use herself boldly, working with and through her own body, to be able to better connect with and comprehend her client, ultimately allowing her to 'fall into the place where her client is'.

Accept your limitations and self-care

Therapists need to be aware of possible limitations impacting their work by considering how they view F-to-FCSA in light of their existing knowledge, any present gaps, and whether they have the support necessary to work effectively and sensitively with these client groups. Therapists working with F-to-FCSA should reflect on whether they need to be in therapy, as this will enable them to recognise their internal processes and deconstruct the impact of their therapeutic work, including developing an awareness of what is theirs and what belongs to the client. Engaging with such complex issues can lead to health concerns; therefore, it is essential to acknowledge that there may be times when one needs to reduce client work and seek support.

Guidance for supervision

Supervision is an important space for the therapist

The supervisor must recognise and own the act of supervision as a vital space to detoxify the mind for supervisees who work in the area of F-to-FCSA. The supervisor must be willing to prepare and create a safe space in which the supervisee can let go and process the complex and often traumatic material from the sessions, so that she can continue her work with more congruency and clarity. The supervisor must understand that the supervisee might become heavily impacted by the work and that, as a result, they might have specific needs related to their work.

Honest relationships between the supervisor and the supervisee

The supervisor should ensure that the supervisee does not experience fear of bringing up and processing various issues directly related to either her client work or personal issues evoked by the arduous work. It is essential that even the most challenging circumstances are processed in supervision, without the supervisor becoming 'shocked' and/or judging the supervisee. The supervisee who is a survivor of F-to-FCSA should feel safe enough to disclose this to her supervisor and be supported if the countertransference and transference become challenging to process.

The supervisor must be knowledgeable about FCSA issues. It is indisputable that the supervisor should be skilled in F-to-FCSA and capable of providing state-of-the-art services; equally important is that the supervisor instils confidence in the supervisee. The supervisor's experience prevents situations where the supervisee feels compelled to educate them about F-to-FCSA.

Advice for future research

There are several research areas of interest that I wish to recommend for future consideration. These are:

1 Researching the long-term effects of F-to-FCSA and the possibility for intergenerational transmission of trauma/abuse is critical.
2 Researching the situation of transgender survivors is relevant. Questions such as how F-to-FCSA might impact gender development/identity would be significant to investigate.
3 More research, adding to the existing ones, into F-to-FCSA within non-Western European culture. My rationale for this type of research is that I lived in various African countries for many years and met women who claimed that female relatives ritualistically sexually abused them. Such research would certainly be invaluable.
4 Broadening the research into F-to-FCSA and examining the factors underlying the motivation behind the therapists' choice to work with these client groups would be useful. This would engender a deeper understanding of whether and how the therapists' past and/or recent experiences may have motivated them to work with F-to-FCSA.

Epilogue

Trapped (Getu, 1977)

An eternity
I have tried
To open the door

Knocked
Banged
Kicked
Wailed

The door has a lock
And my hand has the key

Is the lock too big
And the key too small
Or the lock too small
And the key too big

The whole day
I have tried
To open the door

And when the evening comes
Hear!
Hear!

Steps going to heaven
Steps going to hell

And steps somewhere between
Deep in my heart.

Since I wrote this poem as a teenager, I am no longer trapped. I have opened and closed many doors. But one of the most precious and surprising doors I have ever opened is this book. I hope its wide-open doors have led you deeper into the path of the care, empathy, and understanding of both the perpetrators and the victims of F-to-FCSA.

Index

For Product Safety Concerns and Information please contact our EU
representative GPSR@taylorandfrancis.com
Taylor & Francis Verlag GmbH, Kaufingerstraße 24, 80331 München, Germany

9 781032 999784